CW00482214

# For the love of Country Sports

# By

# Linda Mellor

This book contains stories and individual accounts about
the countryside and country sports: fishing and ferreting,
deer stalking and gundogs, clay and game shooting,
rabbiting and game cooking, falconry and wildfowling.

*Linda Mellor*

**ISBN:** 9781082022616
**Imprint:** Independently published

For the Love of Country Sports

This book is dedicated to my parents, Janette and Lawrie, and their unfaltering commitment to give my sister, Lorna, and I an active, outdoors childhood, and for passing on their love and respect of animals, and to my friends and acquaintances, and all country sports enthusiasts around the world.

.

*Linda Mellor*

# Introduction

How often do we get the opportunity to share why we love country sports? Yes, we have groups, connections, friends and followers on social media but how frequently do we talk about the love?

In recent years, there was an increase in companies giving products away to be shared on social media in the hope a young, attractive face and slender body increased sales. The country sports sector is diverse, it embraces all ages, shapes and sizes. In my job, as a writer and photographer, I have met, and spoken to hundreds of people about their country sports involvement. There's a passion and a pride in their voices when they talk about their favourite stalk, a long distance retrieve, an exploding clay, a beautiful cast across the river, fishing from the shore on a wild, windswept day or cooking a delicious game dish.

It's not about looking good in your colour co-ordinated gear, or catching the light for your best pose with a shotgun over your shoulder.

It's all about the love…

*Linda Mellor*

## Linda Mellor

I grew up in Fife, with my parents, and younger sister. Spending time outdoors played a major part in my family life, and dogs and horses were a deliberate inclusion by my parents as they were determined to give us the best possible start in life by filling our lives with lots of countryside-based activities. We had labradors in the house from when I was only months old, and they were trained by my dad, and worked through the shooting season and competed in tests during the spring and summer months.

Our family life was an outdoor one, I was about eight when we got our first pony, then quickly progressed to bigger ponies. I recall reading the Silver Brumby books and drawing horses in my sketch pads. I have fond memories of the many gallops my sister and I had along the silver birch lined old railway track we called the ash path, and of the canters through the woodland and jumping over the fallen trees. The forests were magical places, bathed in beautiful light with pockets of velvety green grass and full of animals.

They were fearless and fun times, we held on to our ponies as they raced along the paths (and probably where our appreciation for the thrill of speed started).

If we fell off, or were bucked off, we jumped back on. We wore jodhpurs, riding boots and riding hats, there was no

1

special equipment and we were never daunted by mad ponies.

We progressed to horses, but then, around the age of 16, I left the horsey world. As much as I loved being around them, and still do, I did not have the passion to sustain an interest in keeping and riding horses as my curiosity for the wider world took over.

In addition to horses, we supported my dad competing in gundog tests around Scotland. It was an adventure going to big shooting estates, we ate picnics prepared by my mum, enjoyed the competitions and cheered on my dad when he won, and he often did. One Gamekeeper, and Judge, used to joke about putting a road block on the A9 to stop my dad heading north and scooping up the prizes. The gundog tests were great fun: family days out, there were no cliques or back-biting, and we looked forward to them. The long drives were never boring, we returned home late on Sunday afternoons exhausted, with more rosettes and trophies to add to the collection.

Going pigeon shooting with my dad was exciting, and like everything outdoors, it felt like an adventure. I was always in awe of the 12 bore boxlock ejector he shot with, and shared his sense of achievement when we took the birds home. My childhood memories have faded but I can recall l felt a little miffed if my dad and the dogs went out shooting, and I was left behind. I remember, the dogs had a different 'outdoorsy' smell on their coat, and of standing at the kitchen sink as I plucked ducks, and tried not to rip the skin. The feathers had a light, oily waterproof protection, and probably the most vivid recall I have is of the stunning colours.

One cold and damp Saturday, late afternoon, my sister and I were huddled into the tall, thick rhododendrons bushes waiting for the pigeons coming back in to roost on the ground belonging to one of our dad's friends. It was exhilarating staying quiet, and out of sight, as we held onto the hope the pigeons would appear soon, but as the light faded and the temperature continued to drop, our excitement started to wane. My dad stood to the right and ahead of us, camouflaged by the leaves. Our dog sitting to heel. We all looked skywards. Suddenly, a silent, lone pigeon flew over our heads, applied the brakes, then dropped into the trees behind us. It was followed by many others, the sky was full of them. My dad was shooting, reloading, shooting, reloading. In the excitement, we lost our ability to stay quiet, and shouted 'Dad, there's one!' 'Dad, there's another one!' There were pigeons dropping from the sky, the dog retrieved as many as he could, and so did my sister and I.

Often, our holidays would be in the north of Scotland, the excitement I felt then upon seeing the vast open spaces is how I feel today when heading to the highlands, aged 54. As a family, we still carry our memories of a holiday in a shooting lodge at Loch Carron, I am unsure how old I was, maybe nine or ten. We rented the entire floor, it had four bedrooms, sitting room, and kitchen. One of the bedrooms had a horsehair mattress and my grandmother (she often came on holiday with us) was keen to have that room because she wanted to sleep on the mattress, it was something she hadn't done since she was a girl growing up in the first quarter of the 20th century. I recall seeing the huge salmon that lurked in the rock pools at the bottom of the garden, and going shooting and fishing with my dad. I still have a clear image of our dog enjoying his marrow bone bought from the local butchers. He picked up the bone and walked over to where we stood to watch my dad fish. He looked over the edge, and accidently dropped his bone into the water, and scared off the fish.

My dad remembers the midges and going fishing in the evening but not being able to tempt a bite from the huge fish. My mum recollects the hooked appearance of the lower jaw on the salmon, and my sister and I in our yellow and orange cagoules and the midge bites on our skin, stopping at the elasticated wrists cuffs and hoods. My sister, Lorna, recalled the path down to the river, the fish and the pathway across the other side of the river going up into the hills.

Over the years, during the shooting season, I would tag along with my dad to shoots. It was a great feeling being out all day, meeting other people mostly adults, and many were eccentric characters. Looking back, I understand why I embrace adventures because each day outdoors was exactly that. I got to know the workings of a driven shoot, and why cohesive team work was essential to the success of the day. We'd hold the line and shout 'over' as we pushed the birds towards the guns. Often, lunch was eaten in a drafty farm outbuilding, we pulled straw bales around into a circle to sit on, then open up the lunch bag to explore the delights hidden within the tinfoil. Food never tasted so good, a cup of tea or coffee from the steaming flask tasted oddly different to the ones made at home, nevertheless, it was hot and refreshing. The dogs would sit around, ever hopeful of something more interesting than a bonio.

Looking back, I am not sure how my dad was able to fit everything in, but he did. Both my parents worked, and if my mum finished before my dad she walked the dogs. Countless people spoke to her on the dog walks, they asked about the well-behaved Labradors, and she'd tell them they were trained gundogs. People were in awe of her effortlessly walking three dogs to heel.

I moved to London in my early 20s, and regularly drove back to Fife to visit my parents, and during the shooting season I enjoyed to a day out on a local shoot, usually Crawford Priory, with my dad. A shoot day was a good test for any potential new boyfriend, to see how he shaped up in the beating line. It certainly filtered out the moaners! I wish I had used it as an indicator for a suitable husband, because looking back the only shoot day my ex-husband attended he complained about being outdoors and feeling cold!

Boxing day was always a shoot day, there was a great atmosphere: high spirits and fun. We all had a feast at lunchtime with lots of Christmas lunch leftovers, cold turkey, ham, stuffing all tasted great as cold sandwich fillings. Occasionally, hampers were brought out, tins and boxes of biscuits and Xmas cake did the rounds. The shoot days were a great antidote to a London-based career and also fine fodder for my caricature pencil sketches. There was a steady flow of fun stories: rubbish shooting and lots of misses, people falling over or into water, dog tales, long distance retrieves, and syndicate members falling asleep while out on early morning pest control.

In my mid-thirties, I escaped city life and moved out to the Cotswolds, changed careers and established myself as a photographer. I lived in Devon then Cumbria, and started writing and combined it with my photography. I worked within rural topics, news, and women's interest. A move back to Scotland in my 40s, prompted me to direct my focus at country sports.

Over the years, I have seen many changes within country sports, met thousands of people from all over the world and found the majority a delight to work with. I have made many great friends and built an impressive network of experts across the industry. One aspect I recognised as a recurrent theme was the passion people had for their particular sport, be it river, loch or sea fishing, clay or game shooting, gamekeeping, wildfowling, falconry, deer stalking, dog training, beating, picking-up, ferreting or running their own shoot, and the list goes on.

I was brought up to believe there were no barriers and was encouraged to take part in anything I wished, and being female had no bearing upon my participation. When I was growing up, I regularly saw women training dogs, and competing in gundog tests and working their dogs on shoot days, but it was rare to see them shoot. For centuries, there were options for women to get involved, look mythology, in history and record books. There are a multitude of illustrations and reams of literature featuring women fishing, hunting and hawking. So why were there so few taking part in the 1970s and 80s?

Social media opened up country sports: a useful tool to promote what we do, to attract others to come in and have a go. Country sports welcome all, they are no longer exclusive clubs and networks for the wealthy, upper classes. There are sports available to suit all budgets. If you want to go deer stalking it doesn't have to be a royal stag or a medal class buck, doe and hinds are part of a professional cull plans, you don't have to shoot driven grouse, there are plenty walked-up days, driven pheasant or partridge, you can fish for salmon on many rivers not just the world renowned beats, go for grayling, wild brown trout in the hills, sea trout, or head to the coast and give sea angling a go. You just need to dig a little deeper to find something to fit your funds. The big shooting organisations have done, and continue to do, a fantastic job opening the door to all the countryside events and conservation lead activities.

7

Over the last two or three years there had been an increase within the industry of companies using the sector as a promotional platform. The selfie addiction had a use after all! Firms gave out products to people with popular profiles, in the name of increased brand awareness and follower numbers. All too often the themes involved pretty young things decked out in new clobber, and many lacked the gravitas, and were delightfully vague on country sports expertise. But if they looked glam and gorgeous they won followers and more gear from their sponsors. Numerous country sports social media channels became saturated with glamourous images, yet were barren of genuine people who had a passion for country sports. drowned out by fluttering eyelashes, pouty lips and carefully co-ordinated outfits.

In 2017, I took part in brand awareness and promotion campaign with deer stalking outfitter and clothing supplier (UK distributor of the Hillman brand), Venator Pro Ltd. I worked closely with their Norwegian MD Kenneth Larsen to raise the company profile. It was an exciting journey and one I will treasure for the rest of my life, because Kenneth taught me to shoot a .243 rifle.

My lifelong interest in Roe deer was ignited by a trip to the cinema to see Bambi with my mum, I was five. Since then, I've been out on hundreds of deer stalks alone with my camera, or I accompanied others. Pulling the trigger was the only part alien to me.

After an extensive classroom-style induction to stalking and a visit to the range to shoot targets, I accompanied Kenneth on an early morning outing to a Perthshire estate, and shot my first roe buck as part of a professional deer management plan. We field-tested the clothing and footwear on our regular stalks, and shared the outings online.

The 2am rises, the cool autumn dawns and the snowy day breaks were worth every effort. First light is a magical time, an opportunity to pause, take a deep breath and be thankful. To feel the fresh dawn air on my skin and the breeze blowing through my hair enhances the wonder of the world we are lucky enough to share with mother nature.

This book was put together to share some stories of who, what, where and when our hearts opened to the outdoors.

It is all about the love….

Linda Mellor, July, 2019.

## Jonathan Davis

It was an early night, my new waterproofs, woolly hat and gloves were all laid out on my bedroom floor and I just couldn't sleep. My mind was racing at a thousand miles an hour, I was so excited but at the same time was scared of doing something wrong. The following morning, I was going stalking for the first time. I was eleven and I was going with my Dad.

This in itself may not sound very exciting but for me, it was everything. I didn't get to spend much time with my father as a youngster, he was often out well before I woke up and wouldn't be home till it was dark. Although I would go out and help at the weekends to fill the feeders or just ride about in the old 4x4, my parents were determined that my schooling should come first and I wouldn't end up as some feral child that spent more time messing about with Pheasants than learning my ABC..

I wasn't actually excited about seeing any Deer, I was just happy that I was going to spend time with him, I felt like I was a man. I'll never forget walking down that dry irrigation ditch in single file, Dad leading the way, rifle over his shoulder, an old haversack on his back and me following up, desperate not to trip over in my wellies that were always two sizes too big. We moved up out from the ditch and laid in some long grass with the sun just coming up in front of us. I didn't want to be anywhere else. Watching the day wake up, the sound of a murder of

Crows lifting from the distant woods, several Rabbits out in the field oblivious to our presence and what seemed like a hundred Sparrows dancing in and out of the hedgerow behind us.

The countryside for me has always played a huge part in my life, apart from a spell, randomly, in the Submarine Service, which couldn't be a bigger departure from what I was used to, I've almost always spent every moment I could outside. I love the romance of the countryside, soaking up any knowledge I can from anyone willing to impart their years of experience. Most of the people I knew growing up were old farmers or keepers, fishermen or good old country boys. I was always to be found pestering them in a potting shed as a youngster, ever to know everything they did.

We live in a manmade environment. Big square fields, bordered by hedgerows, carefully managed woodlands, manicured rivers and banks, and because of this, we, as man, have a responsibility to manage the wildlife that inhabits that environment. Years of meddling from government, introduction of lost species, protection of others, all puts pressure on nature. It's up to us to keep a healthy balance and that's what gets me out of bed every morning, a desire to leave the countryside each day in a better state than I found it that morning. Even little tasks every day will make a huge difference over a season.

Autumn is my season of choice. Many people see it as a time to prepare for a cold, miserable winter. Not me, the riot of colours, watching the wildlife step up a gear and prepare for the forthcoming season, cool, misty mornings and that anticipation of the first frost so I can pick the sacks of Sloes I need to keep everyone well-oiled over Winter. If you ever want me and can't find me, just drive to a field and wait. I'll be along shortly.

Alex Vankov

'I was born in 1984 in Russia, in small city near space station Baikonur. My father was an Air Force Colonel in the USSR. As you can imagine, my life was like being in the army service, things like discipline, punctuality, respect and hard work were my lessons on daily basis. At the same time as my father was a military man, he also was a huge nature lover, keen hunter and fisherman and these are the very best things I remember as a kid, a teenager and young adult.

I was four years when my father took me to my very first hunt, it was early duck hunting at dawn. The men in the shooting party were different from all others, they all had something special about them, something made them best friends. They were making jokes and telling stories all the way to the hunting ground. Later in my life, I understood that the special something was their true friendship. Friendship with no obligations or social status, they were just men who loved being out and spending time with other likeminded people and enjoying their life, and the moment of being outdoors in the wild.

I remember the times when my father would come back from hunting trips and I would climb over the pile of his clothes, looking at the cartridge belt, knives, and heavy, wet boots and of course, the quarry which was packed in the backpack. We hunted in the swamps, woods and steppe (eco region), we fished on the lakes, rivers an ponds.

13

I guess it was then, when I was four years of age, I understood what the true happiness meant.

After USSR broke up and my father retired in 1991 we moved to Latvia and this is where I spent my teenage years. We were hunting in no time at all, and as it turned out, in Latvia hunting was a very popular thing to do.

Growing up on our family farm, things like hunting, fishing and outdoors activities were unavoidable, so I got good at it. I found the Latvian hunting styles and approaches were a bit different from Russian ones, but what got my attention and amazed me was people were exactly the same. It wasn't important that we just moved in, it wasn't important that we had an accent, the most important thing was that we were hunters and that was all that mattered. Being involved in hunting trips in Latvia was great experience for a teenager, again lots of stories from old hunters, lots of tips and advice, the most helpful were the truckers, they are the ones I spend the most time with. It was fascinating how they would read the trail left by an animal or how they would anticipate the weather and conditions. These sort of skills would be passed on from father to son for generations and no-one can put a value on that knowledge.

In 2005, I came to UK, with no English to communicate, and no friends to go to, nothing. I had nothing and no-one. Hunting was the last thing on my mind, it was something out of my reach. I would dream about hunting based on my memories and the fact that pheasant, rabbits, pigeons and even deer would walk on the side of the road and calmly graze on the fields. I had no idea that one day I am was going to write these words. As my father back in 1991, I was lucky enough to meet a man who became my best friend, we got on so well that we were hunting and fishing at every opportunity (a lot). I have hunted many animals in Latvia, but my best trophy by far was Kentish seven-pointer roe buck which I harvested a day before my birthday with my best friend guiding me. Because of hunting I've met so many amazing people and made so many great friends.

If you ask me what is the hunting, or why you do it, well..! Someone said: "A hunter always be the hunter, and no matter what, he will always have an aim in his life."

I am the living proof that love for hunting and outdoors drives people forward. Hunting pushed me from strength to strength, I have my FAC, then an open ticket, DCS level 1 and 2 came straight after and, later I got qualified as an NRA range conducting officer. Now I am writing hunting articles for Russian and Ukrainian Hunting magazines, and others. Hunting gives people confidence and power to succeed anything there is in front of them.

For as long as I can remember, I wanted to be able to call myself a hunter, and now other people call me that.
'Настоящий охотник, всегда остаётся охотником''

## Mai Gray

'An unlikely story, but my fly-fishing adventures started in upstate New York whilst visiting my in-laws in New York city. I had never held a fly rod in my life let alone cast a line! That was back in 2010. On my return to London, I decided that fly fishing was a sport I wanted to take up and so booked casting lessons.

From there on, I started out fly fishing on rivers in England, Ireland, Wales and Scotland. I also took up loch fishing and lake fishing with a lot of time now spent in Scotland. I then decided to learn fly-tying which is another aspect of this wonderful sport which I love to do.

Fly fishing for me is so much more than just fishing! In the right moment and place, there is much to observe, feel, and be humbled by. I love that when you are wading, you can feel the flow of the water against you, you can feel the breeze on your face, hear the wind in the trees, observe insect hatches, listen to birds and wildlife sounds– everything slows down - your body is in rhythm with your surroundings. There is a rhythm to fly fishing and once you are tuned in, this for me becomes meditation or therapy. And the beauty of fly fishing is that it can take you to so many places in the world!'

## Amanda Murray

'I got started clay shooting because I saw an advert on Instagram for National Ladies Shooting Day (NLSD) in 2017, and thought I'd go along and see what it was all about. I have been a beater for about 10 years, my husband is a keen shot of both shotguns and rifles and I'd shot his shotgun at a ground once or twice. I grew up in East London, apart from shooting gat guns at cans in the garden with my brothers that was the extent of my exposure to guns.

My instructor on NLSD was great and so were the other ladies, a very relaxed environment, light-hearted, fun and just a little bit competitive.  It turned out that I was very comfortable with a gun, and I was able to hit clays, I straighted the last stand (I didn't even know what that meant until it was explained to me) and I trotted out with a rosette and prize for my efforts. I had the best day, on the way home I decided I wanted to do that again and applied for my Shotgun License later that week.

I attended a few more organised shooting events, I met an instructor, Paul Loveday, who has taught me a great deal.

I started shooting more regularly and attended a few private events at different clay clubs and grounds with my husband and friends I'd met through shooting. I joined a clay ground in Suffolk and joined a local clay club, which I never even knew about. The more I shot the more

17

confident I became and the more opportunities I've had to develop.

Starting into the Game Season last year, I spoke to Steve Reynolds the Game Keeper, where I've been beating for years. I asked if I could shoot on Beaters Day and if I could join the small shoot for some of the Beaters that he runs independently. I was really keen to try my hand at game shooting while appreciating that it's quite different from shooting clays. Following a walk around with Steve and a conversation about safety, beaters, gun position, and all things peg related he agreed to let me shoot.

This was so important for me and will always be so very memorable, on the first drive on the first day I shot a high hen pheasant with my 20g Miroku, stood alongside my friends that I have beat with for years. My husband was in the beating line that day and emerged through the trees to see me holding my bird aloft. I was so pleased and proud that everything I'd learned and had been told came together. I was also relieved, as I'd been informed by my fellow lady beaters, that morning that I was representing womankind and they expected me to do well and not let the side down. So no pressure at all. I shot two more birds that day and was thrilled to bring all three home. I spent about 40 minutes plucking the hen bird and I roasted it for dinner the next day in with some finely cubed root veg, a liberal sprinkling of rosemary at least a pint of homemade gravy and a mountain of crisp golden roast potatoes. I spent longer than I needed to prepare the whole meal, but I felt as I always feel when I've taken an animal, a degree of responsibility in doing things properly or honourably. It was a superb meal and was probably the best tasting pheasant I'm ever likely to eat.

The remainder of the season saw me watching other guns, how they shoot, and just generally being in awe of some bloody good shots. Understanding what it means to take a shot and when to leave a bird, what's too low, what's beyond your ability and what's your neighbours' bird. This season I have shot my fair share of pheasants and my first Partridge which I shot stood with my shooting chum Rhiannon. It was on a fantastic ladies day in Cambridgeshire which started with bitterly cold wind and snow on the ground. A bunch of very keen ladies wearing inordinate amounts of clothing and huge fury hats all huddled together in the back of an ex-army transporter. It was an exceptional stand on the third drive of the day which we shared and shot in turns. Rhiannon shot her first partridge moments before me and I was so thrilled for her, she'd been wanting to shoot a Partridge for as long as I had. I took my stand and caught a Partridge as it crossed above a line of small trees, I was absolutely elated when I shot mine.

I encourage as many people as possible to try shooting and have taken several friends and colleagues to clay grounds. I absolutely love shooting, whether its clays or live game both are equally rewarding for me. My only regret is that I came to the sport as late as I did at the grand old age of 41, I so wish that I'd found it earlier'.

## Doug Wheeler

'I'm a little like Jekyll and Hyde when it comes to my love for country sports. Not that I drink dubious concoctions, except a tipple of sloe gin on a cold day, but that the sports I participate in are complete opposites in practice.

I love the tradition of every aspect of driven game shooting, from beating, to picking up, to be stood at the peg, and to enjoying good food and drink at the end of a day's sport. I have been fortunate to have a go at all these parts of what makes up the day, and find equal pleasure in each. The social side of game shooting is what in my opinion makes it so appealing. From arriving in the morning, often before light to prepare the tea and have a bacon sandwich cooked in the shoot hut, it is all small parts of building a good day and the anticipation of what the day will bring is like Christmas morning for me.

The banter amongst the beaters, picking up team, and often the guns can be cruel but all in good nature, and with laughter being the best medicine, a good laugh will make the day so much more enjoyable. This is what I love, the connection amongst like-minded people all participating in their passion. The spectacle of the day is also what makes it so special, seeing everyone in their tweeds, bright shooting socks and caps, dogs scurrying around excitedly, or looking stern as they sit patiently with noses sticking over the tailgate of vehicles, a hip flask being passed around and enjoying a fine Cuban cigar, all these aspects when mixed with strong flying birds, clinical shooting and excellent dog work never fail to bring a smile to my face. The scent from the first fired cartridges of the first drive is on par with the smell of freshly baked bread, and seeing soaring pheasants and rocket like partridges testing the guns after breaking cover makes all the hard work from the rearing season and late nights protecting the flock from predators well worthwhile.

The après shoot as I like to call it is also a huge factor in my love for driven game shooting. Good food and wine mixed with stories of the day are etched into our memories at these occasions, and sitting by an open fire in a country pub is something I will never tire of.

So, as much as I enjoy the whole celebration of driven game shooting and all its glitz and glamour, my true passion is deer stalking, an activity carried out alone and in almost silence, a full 180 degrees away from driven game shooting. To me, there is nothing more enjoyable than sitting in a high seat or silently walking through the woods watching the countryside wake up, or settle down for the night, it is truly magical. I find deerstalking to be almost cathartic, and it gives me time to ponder and arrange my thoughts, relax my worries and have some well needed peace and quiet. On occasions I feel as if it enters me into a zen like state, it sharpens your senses and heightens your awareness, you start to hear every rustle from the wind through the trees, and every snap of a twig, and your eyes pick up the slightest movement through the trees, or notice when something looks out of place. Many deer have been spotted by the slightest flick of an ear, or shake of the tail as stalkers will look for the most minute signs of life amongst the woodland vista.

Morning outings are a time to listen to the dawn chorus, watch shadows cast by the bright moon change into those created by the rising sun, and see the grey colour of twilight magically turn into wonderful rich greens.

Evenings bring a whole different feeling, there is a sense of being very aware of the time, with darkness approaching a sense of urgency sneaks into play, and as the light fails your eyes often play tricks and features you have been looking at during the outing suddenly all look 'deer shaped'. The deer seem more relaxed in the evening, almost as if they are aware that the cloak of safety that comes with darkness is soon to wrap them in for the night, the time where their superior sense of smell and stealth like movement will allow them free movement while we sleep.

It is the connection to the countryside that I feel is so special with deerstalking, and any stalker worth his salt will be practicing field craft, looking for tracks and signs which point to the presence of deer. Hoof prints or slots, well worn trails or racks, and tell-tail hairs on barbed wire all are indicators, along with frayed saplings and browse lines on trees, a well-trained deer stalker will notice all these without actually having to 'look' for them if that makes sense? When you suddenly start to see these signs, and then see deer it makes your effort all worthwhile, and I

23

get so much enjoyment and a sense of accomplishment when all the elements come together, reading the wind, moving without noise, and getting close enough to take a shot after following tracks and signs is an immense reward.

Ultimately a freezer full of delicious venison and a trophy for the wall is what most people are after, but I wouldn't get enough from that, I love the memories that are created in a moment from the stalk, the surroundings and the results.

Both disciplines have given me so much happiness over the years, although whereas the driven game shooting is a socially shared pleasure, the more personal reward from stalking is more satisfying. It is man versus beast, reliving mans primal urge to hunt and provide meat for his family, and it is a test of your patience as much as a test of your ability with a rifle.'

## Audrey Watson

'As an ecologist, I have always loved the countryside and have spent all my working life in the countryside industry – as a Countryside Ranger, an ecological adviser, forester and a recreation consultant and now work as a Deer Officer. I think it must be in my genes as my maternal grandfather was a forester and my father began his working life as a farmer then re-trained as a biologist.

I didn't actually pick up a gun or become involved in shooting until I was in my 30s, mainly due to lack of opportunity. None of my family were shooters and, growing up in a Scottish New Town, I didn't actually know anyone who went shooting and at University my first introduction to shooting sports was American-style! I did my Masters degree in Forestry at Pennsylvania State University and, come the end of November and the opening of the buck season, the building just emptied! I was intrigued as to why and soon came to realise the reason that "buck-fever" is so named but I was interested to hear the stories from colleagues on their "hunting" exploits and their "bird dogs".

It was still a few years before I actually took up shooting, although I lived and worked in the countryside, I still didn't really know anyone who shot until I met my husband. He got me into deerstalking as I accompanied him on his stalking trips to the north of England and quickly decided that I wanted to give it a go too. How someone like me who can't stand the cold, can't sit still and can't keep quiet for very long ever got into deerstalking still mystifies me! Nevertheless, I did the Deer Stalking Certificate level 1 qualification in 2004 and have never looked back. I bought my first rifle - a 6.5 x 57 - then, after a year or so, bought a .243 as ammunition was easier to come by! I now shoot a Tikka T3 Lite in 25.06 and absolutely love it. It is light enough to carry round all day and does the job brilliantly! In 2010, I passed my DSC Level 2 and, in 2018, became one of the few women Approved Witnesses and can now witness for other people who want to do their Level 2.

I have stalked in various parts of the UK, Croatia and New Zealand and my hobby has now become my job. As Deer Officer for BASC, I advise people on all aspects of deer management but, even better, I can take members out on our leased stalking ground in Norfolk. Finding deer for them and getting them to successfully take the safe shot is one of the enjoyable aspects of the job, especially when the client is new to stalking and just starting out on the journey. They'll always remember their first deer.

While I have used a rifle for over 15 years, I am reasonably new to shotgun shooting. I did first try clay pigeon shooting over 10 years ago but my main forays into shotgun use were shooting on the annual beaters' day on our local shoot and I soon discovered I couldn't use one very well! Throughout the season, while waiting behind the guns to pick up with my working cocker spaniel, I'd watch them shooting and try to work out how they were shooting, and wonder what it was that I was or wasn't doing that was making me miss so many. That odd day or two at the end of the season really didn't give me the practice and the experience I needed to improve.

However, a couple of years ago, BASC set up its Ladies Shooting section and at the same time, a lovely lady called Louise Alford started running days for women who wanted to get into clay pigeon shooting under the banner the Yorkshire Fillies (now extended to the Cheshire, Derbyshire and Lancashire Fillies and renamed The Fillies). I started going along to her monthly events and, through this and other clay shooting events mainly aimed at women, I have met a fantastic bunch of like-minded women while improving my shotgun shooting and having brilliant fun at the same time.

While I am a confident woman and always been around men, with three brothers and working in the outdoors industry, I can easily see why having ladies-only events like these help to instil confidence in women who perhaps don't want to try shooting as a new sport in front of men, for fear they will be judged, mocked or, worse still, be completely put off the whole experience by misguided comments. I thoroughly enjoy the ladies days but I have the confidence to shoot clays with men as well as women and now do so on average once a month during the summer, do around three simulated days a year and shoot on game days about 6 days each season with a couple of syndicates. There is a great feeling of satisfaction when the men applaud a cracking bird I have shot! I still shoot on our beaters' day on the local shoot and am pleased to say that I do hit a few more birds than I did in the early days!

I love being involved in the countryside sports industry and love to pass on my enthusiasm and, I hope, my knowledge to others. I like nothing better than being in a wood just as the world wakes up – to hear the dawn chorus and see the deer start moving. I may not even get a shot but to see them and the other wildlife is wonderful. I have watched barn owls quartering below me while I have been in a high seat, had one very nearly land on my head and have watched all sorts of animal antics while sitting quietly there. A far cry from the squeals and giggles of a ladies clay day but both make me feel happy to be part of the shooting community.'

## Frank Pearson

'From ferreting to foxhunting, stalking to salmon fishing, falconry to.... I can't think of another F but rest assured I have had a go at it. I can't explain why, it just happened!

As a child we lived in the country and though my parents had little interest in fieldsports (my father did enjoy fishing in later life) I was always fascinated by nature.

I can recall, aged about 9, asking at the library, for books on Hawking – blank looks all round. In the 1950's falconry demos and bird of prey centers had not been thought of. I also asked for books on Big Game Hunting, probably inspired by Hollywood films about Africa because, back then, there TV's were rare. This produced some results though I can't remember titles. I devoured them avidly – and remember- 'Karamojo' Bell was still hunting at this time. I now have quite a collection of African hunting books.

A friend of my father's had been a military photographer during the recently fought war and LOVED guns and shooting. Rabbits were still in plague mode, possibly the main reason for my getting into sport and I often accompanied Ernie, armed with his take-down, Browning semi auto .22 rimfire and saw much destruction done with that little rifle. He was a great shot and told me he had been reprimanded for shooting tin cans off the shoulders of colleagues with his service revolver, when he was in northern India – he was only a little nuts! I remember him

29

shooting a pigeon on the wing with the browning and many bunnies on the hop. The first centre fire rifle I ever fired belonged to Ernie, it was a Winchester model '98 lever action in .44 long and kicked like the proverbial mule-great fun!

At about the same time my father gave me a terrier, an Easter present in my 7th year and I spent most of my spare time roaming the fields and hedgerows in search of fun, with that little dog. My first ever pheasant, a cock, was flushed by this dog from an October oat stubble and flew straight into some overhead electricity wires. I carried it proudly home and was a confirmed hunter from that day on. A year or two later I spotted a big leveret in it's form and leaving the dog sitting I walked around the hare and brained it with a stone, I read, years later that this was an old poaching trick but I had discovered it by chance. I wasn't poaching – was I? An air rifle was soon acquired and nothing was safe from my predations.

Dogs were always part of my life, several terriers followed the first and endless canines since, including 3 packs of foxhounds, countless terriers and Labradors and a succession of lurchers and coursing greyhounds.

I remember so well seeing my first roe buck. Living in the north of England roe had just begun their relentless spread bid to recolonize the UK from their havens in the Scottish borders. I was sitting one summer evening, on the edge of a wood, with my air rifle, hoping for a roosting pigeon.

A magical beast appeared looking, in profile, for all the world, like the fabled unicorn, and stopped to drink from a water trough, about 50 yards from where I was concealed. In a lifetime spent stalking I have never again witnessed a deer drinking ! Within a couple of years roe were being seen regularly on my uncle's farm in Northumberland. This was in the same area where Henery Tegner (author of The Buck of Lordenshaw ) was pioneering roe stalking in the UK. How I wish I had known of him at the time as I had no mentor or even an interested adult to guide my enthusiasm.

One summer holiday – I spent most of my school hols at the farm I determined to shoot a deer. Always a bit secretive, I crept out before daybreak and "borrowed" the BSA Sportsman rifle (a .22rf single shot) which was kept behind the pantry door in the farmhouse kitchen – no security in those days.

I had done my recce's and slipped along a hedgerow to lie-up behind portable hayrack which had been left about 50 yards from a woodside fence after winter feeding.

What seemed like a lifetime passed when I witnessed for the first time that miraculous feat of sudden materialization which roe deer perform so well. I can still recall the hammering in my chest and shortness of breath as I watched my quarry feeding quietly only a few yards away. All these years later the rest is a blur - I must have taken off the safety, squinted through the (open) sights and pressed the trigger.

31

The deer looked a bit surprised at the sound of the shot and ran a few yards before stopping to look back. I had missed?

I was, I think, very confused and don't remember if I reloaded- a chore with a single shot bolt action, but the deer just took a couple more steps and slowly collapsed before my eyes.

I had no one to tell me that a rimfire was totally unsuitable for shooting deer, or that it was unlawful,- It wasn't, as the 1963 deer act was still years away. The gralloch I treated like a big rabbit – I had done hundreds of those.

Half an hour later, sweating and bloody to the elbows I was back at the farm receiving my anticipated bollocking, for, a) killing a lovely animal ( a yearling doe I recall – no close season either) and b) taking the rifle without asking – yes, in that order.

It was worth it! I was hooked, though it was actually several years before I shot another deer. By then I had moved to Berkshire and was working on an estate with a strong fallow population and no control plan – no one had in those days. With some difficulty I bought a 'proper' stalking rifle – an ex army .303 Lee Enfield, 'sporterized' by Parker Hale. His rifle too had only 'open sights'. Young stalkers today seem amazed that we used to go stalking without optical sights!  In the UK deer calibre rifles were almost unknown at that time, outside London or Scotland. I set to work with a vengeance.

Deer stalking in the 1960's was still almost unheard of in England and when deer were shot it was usually by chance and as pests. I moved to the New Forest in 1970 and was amazed to learn that the forest 'keepers (now rangers) had still been shooting, mainly fallow, but also roe, red and sika, in deer drives with shotguns until just a couple of years earlier.

It had been under the stewardship of Arthur Cadman and Fred Courtier that rifles were introduced as tool of choice. Arthur had left the New Forest at about the time I arrived but years later I got to know him in his retirement and he became a good friend. He wrote 'Dawn, Dusk and Deer' and many features for sporting mags in the 70's and 80's- a very knowledgeable man!

I soon exchanged my old .303 for a more modern .243 and having moved firstly to the Welsh borders then on to Scotland, I had close to 30 years of almost uninterrupted stalking, both on the open hill and in commercial woodland. I have never lost the passion, my main regret being that I had no one to show me the ropes in those early years. I try to compensate, now, by helping others who find themselves in the same boat today.

I have been so fortunate having enjoyed wonderful sport and good fellowship throughout my life, mainly thanks to the kindness and generosity of other like- minded people. In addition to hunting, stalking and shooting in the UK, I have been able to hunt, on several occasions, plains game in Africa and wild pigs in Germany.

I have spent too many nights drinking too much whiskey and swapping tall stories and arguing about ballistics, surprise, surprise. I love it all, whilst making so many new friends.

18 months ago, I moved from Scotland to Norfolk. A move which has opened a whole new world of experience with muntjac and Chinese water deer in profusion and by Scottish standards absolutely monstrous reds. There is always something new to learn in the countryside. Don't believe anyone who says they know it all! This week I witnessed a carrion crow carrying a slow worm, which it thought would be a good feast – until it met me!

So, stick at it and make the most of life's opportunities.'

## Fiona Tweedie

'Having been born in a small village in the shadow of the Campsie Hills, I have been surrounded by beautiful rolling countryside my whole life. Pleasantly surreal to me now, I remember excitedly collecting worms from an old rusting bath and minnows from another positioned at the bottom of my grandmother's garden before heading out with my father and brother to one of the many lochs and rivers in my local area. Learning how to set up the lines, cast and wait for the first bite was so exhilarating and still is to this day.

Having been taught by his father, my own was now teaching me. "Special" guarded secrets of what flies and bait to be used had been passed down from generation to generation. After learning all I needed to know about fishing I was then introduced to shooting at the age of eleven. I started out on the beating line, spending my weekends flushing out game to drive it into position of the shooters, in place of, but not a comparable substitute to the working spaniel. Although knowing my father was an avid pheasant hunter, I never considered asking to accompany him on the other end of the barrel. I enjoyed my time on the beating line and having dabbled with some pest control work with my father but I felt intimidated to make the move to game shooting.

Many years later and looking for something new to occupy my time. I found myself silently seeking professional instruction at a nearby Clay Pigeon Centre. After a few lessons I caught the bug, and when my father suggested he come along and join in, he was pleasantly surprised at how good I was. I feel especially lucky to have my father at hand for any questions I may have and I constantly draw upon his wealth of knowledge and experience, and have my trusty springer Ben by my side. When I asked to become part of the pheasant shoot syndicate my father had been part of for many years, the other members were apprehensive, as being a female in a group of men I may disturb the group dynamic. Inviting them to a weekly clay pigeon shoot put their minds at ease.

Working on the land with my father learning how to raise pheasants for the shoot has been enjoyable and challenging. A gamekeeper once told me that, "a pheasant will try to do anything to kill itself!" and "pheasants can fit through the eye of a needle!" I have certainly found this to be true!

The two disciplines of clay and game shooting go hand in hand and translate well unto each other as I have noticed a huge improvement in my pheasant shooting since taking up the clays. My father has also found a new love within the sport, and we can be found most weeks up at the clay ground in competition with each other. Although I would say pheasant shooting and wildfowling have to be my first and greatest passions. My ideal day would be jumping in my father's 4x4 and heading up to the shoot to tend to the birds. The hard work is over shadowed by the enjoyment of spending the time having such a laugh together eagerly awaiting the 1st of October to roll around so we can get out and start the pheasant season. It doesn't take much to make the day special as long as I have company of my father retelling his old stories of his shooting experiences and occasional hilarious antics of him and his friends.

Having entered a new year my goals are to continue honing my clay pigeon shooting skills and entering my father and I into some of the competitions. We will have a good time and no doubt there will be lots of laughs as we compare ourselves against other shooters to see how we shape up next to them.

We will be getting the land and the pens ready for collection of our birds for this year's season. This will continue to fuel our passion for shooting and no doubt give us new stories to regale for years to come over a hot cup of tea in the bothy on the cold and wet shoot days.'

# Ian Gordon

'I was so lucky to have grown up in a time where there were so many fish in the river, so as an 8year old, until I was in my teens, I could not have failed to enjoy salmon fishing, at this time [late 1960s through the 70s], given the opportunity, every youngster would have been the same. But my fishing didn't start with salmon, it started like that of most other lads at this time, with a worm of the end of some nylon I had pinched from my father's fishing bag. No rod needed just a hook and worm, suspended from a willow branch overhanging a nice shaded spot on the river.

As I write this, I can see the river Ugie, a small river which enters the North Sea at Peterhead on the Buchan coast, in most places no more than 40 feet wide, a slow moving river with fragile, undermined clay banks, meandering through the rolling but fertile Buchan countryside with character similar to that of many small East Coast streams. Like all rivers, the Ugie has its own birdlife and particular ecosystem. Coots and Moorhen are common here at this time, their families now fully fledged and on the wing. Sand-martins amassing around the thousands of burrows in the clay banks preparing for the long journey south, the noise of tens of thousands of geese just arrived at Strathbeg, a loch which at that time was home to more than 100,000 migratory birds. Oh boy, the excitement of waiting for those in the morning with my father, the anticipation of this as a young lad! But that's a whole different story. As I think of my first proper fishing memory, I can smell the very distinctive autumnal air, damp, but not quite freezing, smell of the farmyard giving way to that of the cleaner air as we approached the river, a unique and distinctive smell which I now only very occasionally recall, but when I do, I am instantly transport me back to those more than happy times. Scents are a part of fishing which, although seldom talked about, forms a distinctive part of my fishing memories. Anyone who likes fishing through the night until early morning will relate very well to this.

As the old car trundles to a halt, I finally see the river, the pool which has kept me awake half the night thinking about what it may hold for me. Oh, the excitement, not only my hands, but my whole body shakes with anticipation! Finally I'm here.

The morning mist rolling from the river reveals a Dipper on a rock, alert to all around him he sees my silhouette before flying quickly upstream to his next hunting perch. He has left the way open for me to test my fledgling fishing skills on the good numbers of Autumn Salmon and Sea Trout resting under the banks and in the riffles! My morning had arrived. The tension and feeling of expectation builds, and at this time, inexperienced, I have nothing to cloud my appreciation of the day. I don't yet know what are good and bad conditions, at this moment, the enjoyment of my morning, to a large extent, is in the hands my father [my ghillie], for at this time *I'm reliant on his experience and as was indicative of him, he focuses on the positive [It is so important to have a glass which is half full and not half empty when salmon fishing], he tells me all's good.

Water and weather conditions are fantastic and we have no excuse not to catch one or two fish.

This serves to raise my expectations even higher, now at almost fever pitch; I cannot wait to get to my lure in the river, the next few hours will pass in a flash with my mind now thinking of nothing but that moment, that heart racing moment when my worms are consumed and the fish runs upstream. I fumble with hands now shaking, the worms, captured in the damp darkness of the previous evening, snap, as with trembling hands I try to thread them to my single hook, but eventually I have them secured, "the lure" is now as I want it and my trap about to be set!

Having shown me how to deal with a fish should I be lucky enough to hook something, dad walks upstream a little, out of sight, but not far away, leaving me with the rod and, a little like passing one's driving test and driving the car for the first time, I'm free, free to fish the way I want and, pardon the pun, but to put my own spin on things. The worms are launched a little upstream, dropping through the 4 feed deep water column quickly, the round lead weight, roughly the size of a marble bouncing along the shingle bottom dragging the worms behind. Lifting the rod each time the ball stops keeps my worms on the move, then, in a heart stopping moment, the first strike. I feel the worms being taken but something. Another pull, followed quickly by another. With excitement mounting an the fish nibbling, my 8 year old head is telling me to strike, but luckily my father's words are ringing in my ears, wait until the fish moves upstream for striking. With this, feel the line being taken upstream, I lift the rod and to the surface comes a tail, a big swirl, my god, I've got a salmon! DAD! DAD!! The fish plays hard for around 5 minutes before succumbing to the constant strain provided by me and my 8 foot Shakespeare spinning rod. Dad arrives with the net and I have my first ever salmon. A 6 lb Autumn salmon. To say I'm happy is an understatement. As I wrote this I can still smell the fragrance of that morning, the reeds, long grass. I hear the first of the Geese arriving, heading to Strathbeg. How lucky I was to have a father with a massive passion for salmon fishing. From that moment on I knew salmon fishing would play a big part in my life. Little did I know just how big!

This is my first recollection of the important roll experienced people in Salmon Fishing, particularly for those who don't yet have that experience and consequently seek reassurance from those who have. This valuable lesson learned from my father on that damp but bright October morning, I would recall many times in the future, each time reinforcing the fact that, experienced Salmon Fishermen have an obligation to those with less experience, to help make their day enjoyable by inspiring confidence, by "tactfully" passing on knowledge, so as to increase that of their fishing colleagues or clients.

Sadly however, many experienced people are not adept enough to understand the importance and significance of the word "tactfully", sighting only, their personal haul of fish as something for others to aspire to! In fact, this shallow feature does nothing to inspire others to the

41

wonderful sport which is salmon fishing. What they tend to forget is that salmon are very easily caught; if they are there in good numbers and you have the correct conditions any, for want of a better adjective, "idiot" [can be replaced with any expletive], can catch them. The secret is to make sure you are not always the "idiot" and put others before yourself. Only by doing this will the real joys of salmon fishing become apparent and the shallow part of one's nature begin to find some depth. All too often today, the answer to the following question – How did your week's salmon fishing go? Is answered only with a number and not a statement or description!! A growing culture on our rivers, which I'm pleased to say, is foreign to me!

One of my best customers returned recently from a trip to the River Tweed answered the above question by saying - Thank you for arranging this Ian, we had a fantastic 3 days, the fishing, as you described, was different to the Spey, the ghillies were great, the hotel and staff fantastic, we all had so much fun, really enjoying the fishing and those people who made it special. Could you please arrange this for next year?

I added the above to support the great saying in "Scottish" Salmon Fishing, "There's a lot more to salmon fishing than catching fish". Of course it helps but enjoyment is mainly down to yourself and, importantly, the behaviour and professionalism of those around you.'

## Cara Richardson

'Unlike many of my colleagues and friends, I wasn't born into a family of fieldsports enthusiasts. My folks were, and still are, outdoorsy but spent a lot of time sailing so as a result much of my childhood was spent bobbing about in a boat. Oars were one of the first recreational tools I was handed and somewhere there is a crackly cine film of me learning to row in South Queensferry harbour at the age of three.

The first time I ever had my hands on a firearm was at the age of 17. This venture with a .22 rifle was mostly about impressing my handsome 24 year old tutor with my target shooting skills.

I was smitten; both with him and the joy of hitting tin cans and paper targets. Soon progressed to rabbits and then later that year, not long after my 18th Birthday, bagged my first red stag. I haven't looked back, unless to check terrain, cover, the skyline or animals during a 'hunt' of course.

Shotgun shooting and fishing for trout, salmon and sea-fish all quickly followed as new adventures for me around that time of the late 80's. Given the very remote place in which I lived, they were both great fun and necessary to provide fare for the table.

It's amazing how quickly one learns and sharpens up on accuracy when funds are tight and bullets or cartridges are therefore very precious. Back then, some 30 years ago, a female with a shotgun was not terribly commonplace. I joined a Gun Club and won a couple of female clay shooting prizes – nothing to brag about – I was the only girl there!

Since those early days my hunting, shooting and fishing journey has had many highs, a few lows and a great deal of sweaty or soaked-to-the-skin moments. I wouldn't change any of it for a new Perazzi!

I enjoy it. It's as simple as that. Providing food for myself or family; inputting to a vital managed cull; knowing how my meal has lived and died – and the colour of its fur, scales or feathers; enjoying mind-blowing nature and the wild outdoors; the list of positives and reasons why I love fieldsports and fishing are endless.

From the windy ice cold mountains of Scotland to the 50 degree heat of Arnhem Land, I've had some truly wonderful times, and met some fantastic folks along the way. The blisters, cut fingers, forgotten (or eaten by the dog) sandwich pieces, wet feet, frozen fingers, late nights, early mornings, broken bones, midges and other biting barstewards are mostly forgotten.

The memories of THAT big fish, close quarter eagle sightings, charging buffalo, neon beetles, swimming in waterfalls and high bird successes overshadow all the hard work badges. I consider myself very fortunate to have been raised in an age where climbing trees, constructing go-carts, building dens and guddling for trout was the norm.

These muddy juvenile joys seem to have largely been replaced by time spent with chargeable devices.

Thus it pleases me greatly to see youngsters getting outside and learning about our beautiful nature and basic fieldcraft skills. Hence my involvement in a Youth Trust which has a mission statement detailing just that. It's no secret that a carefree rural life of yesteryear is under increasing threat. Those of us who have know this privilege really must defend it for our grandchildren.

Sure, I miss sometimes. Everybody does. Like golf or tennis, you just never know when you are going to hit that next perfect shot and that's a small part of what keeps me going. You miss with 100% of the shots you never fire – so for as long as I'm able I fully plan to keep calm and carry on hunting.'

# Dean Cortan

'I was born in Zagreb 1980, where I finished primary and secondary school and became an electrician, then I went to college and became a civil engineer. I started learning foreign languages at the age of seven, did a lot of different sports, but always loved to be outdoors.

One of my grandfathers loved fishing, so I got my first fishing rod when I was seven, we were always fishing for a predator fish like pike, because the lake had a lot of those, and it was 15 minutes by bike from where we lived. Grandfather taught me how to make our own fishing wobblers. I made mine by hand from old spoons and forks. It was a great satisfaction to catch a fish on a lure I made myself. I was fishing for about 10 years with one grandfather, and went hunting with my other grandfather, who was a gamekeeper. He lived in countryside in the house where my father was born, 100 miles from where I lived in Zagreb. I spent every school holiday there and some weekends, going with grandfather in the woods and controlling the number of game, and where the trees were big enough to be cut down.

Only trees that were big enough and old enough were brought down: logs taken to the sawmill, and the farmers had the smaller branches farmers to keep their houses warm in the winter. New trees were planted every year. Even kids from school were involved in planting trees or picking up acorn and chestnut.

We would put chestnuts on fire for 10 minutes and then eat them, and acorn was put in plantation, watered and in a few years moved into woods for afforestation. My father has two brothers, they are both forestry engineers. Both work in companies that manage woodland and wild game. So I had a chance to learn from them at a very early age. We always had a few hunting dogs; hounds, they were breeds that were local because they were the best for the game we hunted at that time.

That was 30 years ago and 90% of game hunted in front of dogs was foxes and hare. Just a few times a year a wild boar. My grandfather loaded his own ammo, and he had only one shotgun, a side by side, made in Russia. Both my uncle and I have the same. I know there are better ones nowadays, but this as my first firearm and listened to my heart when I was buying it. Hopefully, I will get over and under this year.

When I was 18, I went to school for hunters. One had to be in an internship for a year, before you take an exam. I passed the exam, and got my first hunting dog, German spaniel, whom I named Lun.

I hunted wild boar mostly as a beater, and passed an exam on a blood trail with my spaniel Lun. We hunted over 10 years together and helped on commercial shoots, just for the love of the sport, and a chance to work with my dog.

I passed an exam for grading trophy by CIC standard and was given a licence by the state to do that. I also took an exam for a gamekeeper, and I am doing that in my shooting club as a volunteer.

For almost 6 years now I have had my own company, tourist agency, helping people to organise their vacation in Croatia and countries around it, for hunting, fishing or diving, I always visit the place I will take the tourists before they come.

I enjoy shooting a rifle, and am a member of shooting club. We shoot competition once a year at 300 meters using old rifles, older then I am: models like M48, M98, as long as they are 7,9 calibre (8X57). At this moment I have a GSP, from trail blood lines, he has proved to be a great working dog, and I hunt walked-up bird with him.

When it comes to hunting it is never only about just hunting. I, like most of my guests, like visiting new places, I have hunted in Slovenia, Austria, Slovakia, Serbia, and Bosnia.

Sometimes it is not important what the quarry is, just as long as we are out, in good company, hunting, and after that we have good food, good drinks with locals, and sleep at a nice place like a lodge in the middle of the woods, where hunters sit by the fire and lie to each other about hunting.

I have noticed that people give too much attention to things that are not that important and then they do not enjoy the hunt as they could. So they have put burden on themselves because they believe the brand or the rifle will make them better hunters, or a calibre of a rifle will bring the animal down faster. Use kit that you are comfortable with and that is reliable.

In pursuit for perfect equipment one can loose the goal. For me, the best trophy I bagged are pictures and memories. I try to keep everything simple, and stop as often as I can to smell the roses.'

## Helen Owen

My passion for Wildfowling started when was under 10 years of age. My Father was a Wildfowler and one of the original members of my Wildfowling Club, his Father also a Wildfowler. I grew up with talk of Wildfowling and ate duck and goose on a regular basis so it felt natural to want to be Wildfowler too!

 I regularly spent time on the marsh with my Dad on evening flights, sitting in a Suaeda bush and trying to keep quiet. I was never bored or scared of a dark marsh. The marsh played a big part in my childhood years during Summer months too, with regular trips to swim in the creeks and forage for a bit of samphire for supper. This was all good knowledge for the later years when I joined the local Club, as I already knew the marsh well. I joined in my late teens and spent a year as a probationer before College and part-time evening jobs took over. When I met my husband, we found a mutual interest in Wildfowling and I joined the Club again with him.

I think Wildfowling is a bit like Marmite, you either love it or hate it. Getting up at 3am to set off for morning flight, a walk of a mile across a cold, wet marsh when it's preferably blowing a hoolie, is not everyone's cup of tea.

If you love it, it will be a lifetime passion that will continue to grow each season. It's a lonely shooting sport as a lot of the time you are sat, just you and your dog, either waiting for the sun to come up or the sun to set.

Awaiting the exciting duskiness light which brings the anticipation to a head.

Some flights you will see absolutely nothing or what you do see will be out of range. I can't say this ever really bothers me as to be out on the marsh listening to the nature around me and being so close to it is a massive privilege and something that I will never tire of. When I have a fantastic flight and everything goes just perfectly and I return home with birds in the bag it is something I will probably bore everybody with my tales! The sound of 30,000+ pink footed geese leaving their roost is amazing, the deafening sound of their 'wink, wink' call and beating wings certainly gives you Goose Fever. You will constantly hear it all day after that flight, it just seems to stay ringing in your ears.

Best laid plans can go totally wrong and I've ended up being somewhere I hadn't planned to be and the result was brilliant. I recently had a couple of flights like this, one being a morning flight where I was taking a guest out with me on a day pass. I had watched the Pink Footed Geese and knew where they were flighting and I had checked the tides, which were going to over the marsh that morning so picked a spot I knew I could sit the tide out safely.

Now I'm not used to taking people out with me and got myself a little bit nervous, ended up missing where I wanted to turn midway across the marsh and not wanting to look a fool in front of my guest I quickly decided on a different place.

51

I knew we could sit the tide out and hoped and prayed that a few geese might break off in our direction. We got settled and the tide surrounded us. I could hear the Pinks sitting in quite close so felt hopeful.

As the dawn started to break, the Pinks moved off the way I'd watched them previously with a few passing us out of range but to my delight some Greylag got moved off by the tide seaward from us, flew just wide of us and turned to come straight back to where we were sitting, and looked like they wanted to land on our little island.

I sat tight and let my guest shoot, who happened to miss with both barrels! I have never known geese wanting to land actually on top of me but they wanted to so badly that they came around a second time and unfortunately it was my turn to miss but I was extremely happy that my guest dropped one of the greylags! I later bagged a beautiful drake Mallard. A great morning had by both of us. We then spent the rest of the morning watching the marsh come alive whilst waiting for the tide to drop so we could walk the mile back to the car. I have been hidden up in creeks or bushes and had Marsh Harriers, Owls and even Peregrines pass within feet of me if not over my head. Wildfowling is not just a love of bringing fantastic meat to the table, it's a love of the birds and the surroundings that come with it.

The love of the marsh and its habitat also brings with it a great feeling of wanting to protect it and keep it wild and in its natural state.

*Linda Mellor*

With tourism on our Coast growing and the curiosity and promotion of such unknown places, I fear in years to come that the wildness will be lost.

Our Wildfowling Club will strive to protect it for future generations. Wildfowlers have been present for over a century on the marsh that I shoot and I do hope it continues. To lose it would be devastating but for now I will continue to enjoy every morning, evening and tide flight that I can manage in this wild and desolate place.'

## Duncan Thomas

'One of earliest shooting memories is stood on, a near arctic, Fell side on the Yorkshire/Lancashire border with the Hatton family, aged approximately 6-7 years old, wearing badly fitting wellies, my school sports socks (my only long socks), soaking wet jeans, a leaking "Peter Storm" cagoule, squinting into the eye of an icy hailstorm after being told to tap my stick on the top of a dry stone wall.

The Guns had created a near military-esque ambush and I was part of a seriously cunning plan, a beater, part of a team, with "grown-ups", doing grown up stuff.

We never bagged much on that shoot, I can remember a feeling a great satisfaction carrying an enormous hare from the Moor once and if we bagged a pheasant or snipe it was always a great result, to be celebrated in the Pub. I fired my first shotgun on that shoot, I managed to blow a tin can off the top of a dry stone wall and I was hooked forever.

Within a few years, I had my own air-rifle and was becoming a decent shot with a black widow catty, any excuse to go rabbiting or still my all-time favourite sport, ratting. I carried my Ferrets in an old Doctors medical bag. My first dog was a Large Munsterlander, a genuine "jack of all trades" and between us we were a bag filling team.

We were once chased out of some woodland, ok, I may have got my permissions slightly "confused", the Farmer was on horseback and we had run across two recently ploughed fields desperately trying to get away, he caught up with us, we were exhausted, he leathered us with horse whip, not particularly politically correct or acceptable nowadays but it did us no long term harm. Nor did the worry of the next few weeks of terror wondering if he would see/recognise me at the family house, yes, he was also our milkman.

I soon graduated into shotguns and we managed to secure a small 250 acre rough shoot on the banks of the River Hodder in Lancashire. I had made it, I was now "big time"! We ran the shoot as a syndicate for over 10 years, we loved it, we released a few hundred pheasants, flighted the river for duck and stalked a few roe deer.

We had all the drama's of the small shoot but it was special, I still rue to day we gave it up but I had been offered a role abroad and would be away on and off for nearly 2 years.

Whilst working abroad in Serbia I was offered to join a team of locals on the annual Bear Hunt. How could a chap resist? We were issued with an old rattling Kalashnikov rifle, a single bullet each and off we set walking in extended line, like the longest rough shooting line ever, over 50 of us. My language skills were limited but I could hold my own in basic circumstances by this stage and we ended up in an old bothy type building almost 15 miles from where we had started.

We had a roaring party, (Rakia and cold meats had already been stashed for the feast) and slept where we fell.

The following morning we did the return walk, no bears were hurt in the making of this tale and once back at the bar I asked when they had last seen a Bear, I was told they had last seen one over 20 years ago, it had been shot by a Farmer stealing sheep, sensing my amazement at the fact that the group still went and did the annual walk knowing it was almost impossible that they would ever see one again my guide went on to explain "we cant break the tradition of the hunt and the party". I learnt a lot from this.

The social side of shooting had always been extremely important to me, I'm not bothered about wanting to shoot big bags, 50-150 is absolutely fine and some rough/mini ambush days have been followed by the finest of "debriefs". One of favourite shoots Bolton Hall presents "greedy slippers" for overzealous guns, tennis racquets for low birds and an elaborate but effective fine system, all donated to charity that keeps the line in order. I love it.

My current job sees me looking after the interests of nearly 30,000 shooters in the North of England, It's a very demanding role and I'm lucky to have a brilliant team, and it has allowed me to make a significant effort to one of my most important of personal and professional objectives, Youngshots .

We have taken 1000's of youngsters and given them really positive shooting experiences. I'd be delighted if they all took it up as a hobby but the priority is that they grow up viewing us a decent, nice people. Just as passionate about Conservation as actual shooting.

Our Youngshots have a number of conservation projects and our Lead Youngshots Ambassador Lewis Bretherton runs our now legendary bird box project, 1000's of bird boxes placed in woodland across scores of Game and Clay Shoots, the youngsters have got to learn to do their bit.

I've been very lucky to shoot driven Grouse. I love driven Boar in the cold but I suppose my favourite would be a small pheasant day or duck flighting followed by great mates in a great country pub.

I've been lucky to have been blessed with some incredible dogs over the years, these dogs have taught me far more than I ever taught them and they have certainly got me out of some sticky situations.

My son Ben was lucky enough to have been granted a once in a lifetime experience as a PH in South Africa, he was there for nearly a year.

We went over as a hunting holiday to see him, bringing my Mum and Dad as well for their Golden Wedding Anniversary. We had an amazing time and Ben would have been in his early 20's. He had gone over there as "my lad". On the first morning whilst getting ready to set off for an action packed day I heard him talking to his boss in Africaans, his trackers in Xhosa and taking charge of his parents and grandparents. He was a man, the place had made him, of course we had done our bit, but I'm a great believer in that the extended shooting family and community make the most amazing parents to all our offspring.

I'm 100% committed to ensuring that our children's children enjoy and friendship, craic and bonne amie that I have enjoyed, we must leave a sustainable shooting situation that compliments and enhances the environment.

The shooting community must pull together, there are too many passengers and we must police ourselves ensuring best practice at all times.

Happy hunting all, "what hit is history and what's missed is mystery"…..'

## Lynn Christina Hook

'I must have inherited my love of Country Sports from one of my Ancestors having been born to non-sporting parents. As a child I was always out and had the usual collection of jam jars containing tadpoles, caterpillars and the like. Conkers, chestnuts and, not knowing any better then, picking Bluebells, Snowdrops and other wild flowers. Poppies were good as you could make dollies out of them.

The next step, as with a lot of girls, was horses. First of all ponies, I was lucky enough to live near a forest where you could disappear for hours admiring the beauty of the woods and not see a soul. From there, I went to work in a Racing stable until the need to earn a living took over.

Then I met the person who later became my husband, he taught me about rough shooting, fishing, working with ferrets and dogs. When we married we had terriers and lurchers. The terriers were great fun as were the lurchers, great to watch as they worked. I remember once one of our lurchers put a fox out of some long grass, she took off after it and we took off after her.

There was a man coming the other way on a horse, we must have been a sight to see, all three of us full pelt through the grass. Then there were the Terrier Shows, mostly Hunt shows, where you would meet some of the great old Country characters a lot of whom are gone now as is a lot of freedom to work terriers and lurchers.

61

Next came Birds of Prey, mostly Hawks. As with a lot of beginners it began with a Buzzard who was useless, he just ran along the floor behind you! Then Harris Hawks: they were relatively rare then so up went a breeding Aviary and lots of chicks were hatched. I spent many an hour hand rearing incubated chicks minced chick or rat. This is not for the faint hearted first thing in the morning. The garden lawn always had some sort of bird staked out, Goshawk, Sparrowhawk or some sort of hybrid Falcon. Also, it is difficult to watch TV with a bird being manned down in your living room. Again more friends were made with the same interests. I must say, it is a wonderful sight watching Birds of Prey fly and catch their prey even if only to the lure.

Then came the real love of my life. Driven Shooting.

I was working full time and started going beating on a Saturday. I loved it, the almost military precision. The Beaters were so far flung but all came together at the flushing point. The camaraderie, the people, the atmosphere even when you are freezing cold or soaking wet. All these people that turn up day after day definitely not for the money but for the love of the sport. Someone suggested I get a little Beating dog so an advert went on to one of the gundog sites and that is how I got to know my lovely Irish friends.

One contacted me saying he had a little ESS bitch that was not quite good enough to trial. I took the risk and bought her and the rest is history.

I bought another one from there who was a retired trialer and a Lab from Scotland. This led to me being asked to pick up. At the same time I was made redundant from my job which, when it happened seemed a disaster but was in fact the best thing that happened to me. It meant I could do what I loved full time.

In my time, I have picked up on small shoots, Private shoots and Commercial shoots, which is where I go most of my time now, shoots are all different but all give me the same opportunity, that is, to work my dogs in the beautiful Cotswolds. I work Springers , currently I have 13, one youngster, two retired and the rest are used in rotation as I am out 5 to 6 days a week during the shooting season.

I have to mention my most loved dog of all. Iffy, a non working, Working Cocker, who I acquired when she was three, she sits on the back seat of my Land Rover and toddles along behind all my other girls on the drives. Springers are such happy dogs. I love watching them work, backsides wiggling and tails wagging. They are so pleased when they can bring something back to Mum even if it is something stinky that has been dead for weeks which I balk at taking off them. During the season they pick up pheasants, partridges, ducks and one or two other things that are shot. I get to be an armchair shot although, I can shoot and own two shotguns and a rifle, I prefer to work my dogs and watch the guns.

Summer is catch up time in the garden, plus training the dogs. There is nothing better than watching all the birds nesting, catching glimpses of young wild life as you walk the fields.

I love Country Sports as they take me to a world not a lot of people are privileged to see. The rurality of it all, the people and the traditions. I love nature and wildlife. Just because I can dispatch a wounded bird does not mean I won't try desperately to avoid one on a road. Our house is quite often home to some baby bird/animal being hand reared ready to be released. There are Ferrets at the bottom of the garden and at one time loads of Bantams too, and the occasional litter of pups.

The Country is my life and long may it continue.'

## Ian Robertson

'I was one of the lucky ones brought up by a father who had a passion for country sports and a grandfather, (known to me as Papa), who was not only a country sports man but a massively knowledgeable naturalist. He had spent some of his young life as a ghillie on Invercauld estate which I only found out after his death and when work bought me to this part of the world. Recovering from days off school with the cold or flu were spent walking the back roads around Houston (when it was a small village) learning about the flora and fauna listening, watching, smelling, touching and being at one with the natural world round us, no doubt learning life lessons of patience and discipline learning that patience delivered results with close quarter encounters with foxes roe deer and the birds. Just being close and experiencing the sometimes comical frolicking of these beautiful creatures. I was also fortunate to live my young life in a village with a pack of hounds where I spent many hours working on the knacker run and as kennel boy learning how to avoid evil collies as we collected the fallen stock from the local farms, and developing a love and respect for our canine friends. My lasting memory of the hunting world was bedding down the hounds after a day's hunting and a feed. I loved sitting amongst 20 hounds still steaming in their fresh straw bed.

They would just start to settle when one or two hounds would sit up and began to sing, closely followed by the rest, five minutes of magic sitting amongst completely content hounds steaming with damp, singing their heads off.

My father was an artist at catching fish without a rod, brown trout by hand and salmon with the 'hazel and gold' not the most orthodox fly – a hazel walking stick and gold wire, a rabbit snare tied to a stick. I clearly remember the first time I saw this magical and, of course, illegal feat of skill, and what a skill.

After lying down with his head under the root of a tree on the river bank for 5 minutes waiting for his eyes to get used to the light and until the tails of the fish became visible, my father turned to me and said 'if the tractor in the field comes over this way give my feet a kick boy'. Keen to do my job well, I stared at the tractor working the field while watching the notch being cut on the stick and the snare being tied on. Two minutes later a sparkling salmon of around 4lb came flying out from under the tree root snare firmly around the tail. The urgency of our departure from the scene by a usually placid and cool man alerted me to the fact something about this wasn't quite right! But, oh my god, that was incredible. I would later watch the process in action, lifting the tail with the snare and sliding it over without disturbing the fish, perception of depth being the real skill.

Snaring rabbits and catching fish by hand and stick as a youth on the west of Scotland soon progressed into gun and rod with dreams and stories of Scotland's east and north with rivers full of large salmon, large herds of deer and bags of pigeons that would wear out your gun.

A mornings shooting with my father, Papa and uncle on a Saturday before heading off to play rugby might produce a pheasant a hare and possibly a woodcock but would definitely produce a sore throat from shouting at a half trained dog.

My true love of the multitude of country sports, deer stalking, was however born through another life experience. Sat in an old quarry waiting for rats coming out from under an old mattress with my air rifle I had my first really close encounter with a roe buck. I watched him for what seemed a lifetime at around ten yards, I was mesmerised, grazing browsing and going about his business, occasionally staring straight at me, eyes fixed on me, head bobbing but finally content I was no threat. To this day I don't know what engaged me but I have been fascinated by deer ever since. I can't remember how many deer I have shot or been responsible for guests shooting but I do know that I can justify every shot I have taken regarding sustainability of the species.

Watching roe deer in the rut always makes me think of the contradiction between the general public's lack of understanding and the bambi syndrome and the reality of the aggressive nature of the rutting roe buck or the brutality of the roe doe trying to chase out her previous year offspring.

While fishing for trout on a late July evening I watched an amazing scene of aggression.

I was watching a young roe buck on the opposite bank in his splendid russet coat grazing quietly as I fished down to the tail of the pool. the river was a good height with a deep and boulder strewn fast flowing and turbulent tail.

The young buck suddenly became alert and stared across the river I couldn't see what had got his attention until a large mature buck appeared running at full tilt into the river, he was instantly bowled over and disappeared under the water reappearing and disappearing as he fought the current and the boulders desperate to get at this young upstart. I couldn't believe my eyes or that he would take on the rapids to chase the young pretender of his patch. This he did, eventually emerging on the other bank completely drenched and chasing the young pretender along the haugh, up the hill and away. He appeared back at his exit point a few minutes later breathing heavily and examining his exit point from the river, quickly making the decision to cross back at another point. I have no doubt that he could easily have been killed in the river just to hold his doe and his breeding rights.

Having enjoyed fifty years of hunting, shooting and fishing we have to offer in this country I have to say I have almost gone full circle with regard to where my interest in the countryside lies.

I now enjoy most lying on a wood edge or hill environment on a summer's evening with a fellow countryman letting the wildlife come to us, there may well be reason to shoot a fox or a deer but there is certainly no need.

All the things I enjoyed when I was a wee lad with my papa are now the same things I get out of my countryside experience.'

## Mhairi Ann Hill

'Growing up in rural Aberdeenshire, I was exposed to Country Sports from an early age, my Father, Fraser Troup, was a huge inspiration to me as he taught me many skills I'm now passing on to my two boys, Rex, 13, and Hartley, 8.

My Father taught me air rifle shooting at the age of 8, I have such fond memories shooting for hours in the crisp Scottish air firing at targets, and to add fun he would line up used cartridges it was great fun hitting the brass and watching the how high they'd fly. With red cheeks we'd head home and sit in front of the coal fire and discuss my progress looking at the grouping of my shot targets. I was always determined to improve and won trophies within our local Shooting Club, the Kingseat Fieldsporters. It was there I started to fly fish, I had no idea how five hours looking at the still water would pass so quickly, a fantastic escape to lose the pressure of everyday life: looking at the beautiful scenery awaiting the tightness of the line between your fingers.

The club had five disciplines for me to participate in which were Air Rifle, Clay Target, Pistol Shooting, Fly Fishing and gun dog trials. My Father bred English Springer Spaniels, I loved helping him feed and look after anything between 5-12 in a litter. I'd watch him with a keen eye to gain knowledge on gun dog training something that I'm sure my Dad would agree would be challenging at times.

I progressed heavily into Shotguns and relished the challenges before me with the tuition of my Brother, Scott, I went on to win county competitions in Cheshire and West Sussex. Scott trained as a gamekeeper in Thurso, I'm always delighted to be invited by his syndicate to shoot at Barra Estate Aberdeenshire, a fantastic day out with real characters "The Barra Lads" The camaraderie is so special. On one shoot last year I brought my youngest son Hartley and he stood next to me, I was able to explain the food cycle to him and how fresh the meat would be for our supper that evening. I'm so passionate about country sports and would encourage everyone to get out and give it ago. A simple walk outdoors can be so rewarding in the pressures of today's hectic lifestyles.

After competing I wanted to give something back to Shooting so I qualified as an Instructor and have been offering my advice for over 15 years now down in West Sussex and was overjoyed at winning CPSA Coach of the Year 2016

I'm currently involved in encouraging our young generation away from social media and to enjoy the country outdoors with clay target shooting calling them my Starshots. Seeing the look of elation on a child's face when they hit their first clay evokes memories of my own childhood. Thank you Dad for instilling in me a love of Country Sports. I'll be forever grateful.'

## Ian Shaw

'"Can we go fishing, dad?" This was a common, and almost daily question posed to my father from me at the age of eight. Like in those young years, I live and breathe fishing, but back then reading Mr Crabtree Goes Fishing, Angling Times from cover to cover, and every essay I wrote at school had a fishing or hunting theme attached, no matter how different it was to the theme dictated by the teacher, I always found a way of introducing my passion.

By the age of ten, I was a competent game angler, fishing for salmon and trout on my local River Ribble in Lancashire. My first wild brown trout fell to a dry March Brown on the Brockhall Pool. I was well and truly hooked and my childhood and adolescent years were spent with either a rod or gun in hand. My father had me shooting crows and woodpigeon with an old BSA air rifle with a very unprofessionally sewn down stock on some local permission. My first fishing rod was a home-made (by dad) 6' boat road paired with an Intrepid Black Prince reel! How times have changed, as all who know me, know that I am the ultimate tackle-tart!

Even in my late teens, girls, beer and playing drums in a band (we didn't do gigs, just auditions!) never distracted me from my true love.

In my early twenties I joined the Police Force, and as all who have served know, this is a particularly dangerous and stressful job, which is probably why I became even more immersed in my love of field sports and in hindsight, probably used this as escapism.

It is all about being out in the great outdoors enjoying everything that nature brings. The changing of the seasons, watching the leaves changing colour, and equally important, spending time with great company.

I am very fortunate to have so many like-minded friends to shoot driven birds, walked up shooting and days on the river hunting salmon. Of course a well-earned drink in a local pub afterwards is a must, and I can guarantee that more fish were caught and stratospheric pheasants shot in that pub than ever actually did fall to a fly or shot!

I fished the River Tay early one morning, and within 30 minutes I had seen a magnificent stag attempting to cross the river followed by an Osprey picking a fish from the same pool that I was fishing through. I didn't catch a fish that day, and but it didn't matter! Just to see that spectacle of nature was more than enough for me.

Along with five friends I took advantage of a few days fishing on Park Beat on the River Dee during a first week in February. We hired a cabin and within minutes of arriving, we had managed to fill it with fishing tackle, fly tying equipment, Stella Artois, gin, single malt and anything else containing at least 5% alcohol.

We had decided it was a good idea to retire to bed early for the following days fishing, however at 4am we were still drinking a new creation called Ginto!  It's gin and Vimto, as someone had forgotten to pack the tonic.  We devoured fried Spam and egg sandwiches and wondered why the hell we felt so rough when we were greeted by the ghillie at 8:30am.  I often wonder what he thought of the sight of us reprobates that morning.

That day provided some incredible fishing and one particular fish I caught was a 14lb fresh salmon bearing tailed sea lice.  Although not the biggest salmon I have caught (that stands at 27lbs), it put up a Prima Donna performance and I felt it was going to take me back to sea. I landed the fish after a 15 minute battle as snow began to fall.

Catching that fish really was the dollop of cream in the soup on what was a fantastic trip with good friends, roaring laughter, fishermen's tales and far too much to drink!  Happy days!

Now, I am retired and I have even more time to enjoy these precious days.  I have my faithful young Labrador, Fern, by my side and she is becoming a very accomplished working dog, but most of all a beautiful companion to share these times with.  Her first ever retrieve filled me with as much joy as any high bird I have ever shot, and made me appreciate just how clever these dogs truly are.

All the hard work and training paying dividends and producing a dog that I am so proud of.

I cannot imagine life without being engaged in field sports. It has provided me with fantastic memories, long standing friendships and food on the table.

I don't think there's any coincidence that God allowed the salmon fishing season to commence as the shooting season ends, and the shooting season to start as the salmon season ends!'

## Sarah White

'I was working in a dental surgery as a full time nurse for a few years after leaving college, I was single after a long five year relationship and in my early 20's.

A dear friend noticed I was working harder than I was playing and suggested I went beating on a game shoot in Surrey. "Put your jodhpurs and boots on girl, stop being boring and come and bash some trees with me" how could I resist?

I was apprehensive although I had been an outdoor girl being very sporty when younger, riding and sailing with my family, this shooting thing was never on my radar. However my friend reassured me that if I did not like what I saw then I did not have to go again.

First thing I need to inform any budding beaters is not to wear long riding boots as you slip and slid all over the place. After picking myself up many times and providing a lot of laughs from likeminded people I soon fitted in. The camaraderie was something I was missing and I was hooked very quickly. After a season of beating, I befriended my long term friend who was a gun on the shoot. He often reminds my friends that I walked out of the bushes waving a stick and he was holding his "red hot weapon"!

I was known by my beating friends as dog-less Sarah however I did have my beloved pet rabbit which I kept a secret .Coco was lop-eared and when introducing my friend to Coco I was so worried he would shoot her! Alas my fears were soon distinguished as he was as soppy as me with pets.

After some time we adopted a six month old cocker spaniel called Archie and I was dog-less Sarah no more. A few weeks later we received his pedigree which made me think about training him. Using my competitive nature I started with working tests and then field trials, I never dreamed in a few years' time I would become a gun on a trial. We grew our pack every two years and when my circumstances changed we had five cockers all two years apart. I loved my little pocket rockets and would train every evening after work.

My circumstances changed when I purchased a shooting lesson for my partner's birthday and met my, now, coach, who escorted us around the ground. At the end of the lesson, I asked my coach – "how do you get into pushing buttons?" The look he gave me was priceless!

A few months later I plucked up the courage to contact the shooting ground and they offered me a full-time job after a year being freelance and the rest is history.

I learnt my trade over eight years, said goodbye to nursing, started a new life on my own with my dog, qualified as a coach many times over, learnt to shoot, earned my England and GBR clay shooting Caps, Won coach of the year 2015 and then started my own coaching business.

The opportunities I have been given in this industry have been amazing and although shooting is still seen as a man's world, I was, and still am, the boss to many male colleagues. The chance to join a sport where everybody wants to help you be the best you can and shoot on the same level, where there are no boundaries is unique. If you're ever given the chance to do something out of the ordinary grab it with both hands you never know where it will lead. I have been very lucky and I have always worked in jobs I love but to be working in the countryside, breathing the fresh air every day, watching the wildlife and enjoying the friendship of many, is something I will always treasure.'

## Jamie Stewart

''Jamie, Jamie!' I stirred to see my father at the bedroom door, beckoning me from my duvet. Oh yes, I remember now. 'Do you want to come out for a duck flight in the morning, son?' Yes, please, dad! Seemed a good idea at the time...

After several attempts, where I am sure I had fallen asleep again, he managed to get me roused, up and dressed. I don't know who was more excited, my eight year old self or my dad!

As I write the words, the memories come flooding back in vivid technicolour. The cork screw roe buck, the sublime dawn teal, the steam floating up from the hot coffee on a cold estuary, the smell of ferrets and the seemingly endless summer days at the pigeons. I lost my dad a few years ago, but I still speak to him every day and often recount our many adventures to my own sons and grandsons.

Was it the fact that I enjoyed spending time with my father so much that drove my love of the countryside or was it something deeper? The good old nature versus nurture debate whether human behaviour is determined by the home and parental environment, or by a person's genetic make-up.

Whatever the reason as an eight year old boy, my world was full of firsts.

Hearing the evocative call of Curlew as I lay out at a fox den and the drumming of the Snipe at the close of day. My first Sika stag whistling in the darkness, like some unseen banshee and Red stags roaring so loud that it seems to rattle the teeth in my head.

Even at school, when I went, I was first with my hands up when discussing the natural environment. Maybe not so much for Maths, English and that other stuff...It didn't come as a surprise then that I would chose to follow a career that facilitated the continuation of my passion. Although, it wasn't all plain sailing.

Like most at fourteen, I visited my careers adviser, Mr Stewart. Well Jamie, have you thought what you would like to do after you leave us?. Yes I said excitedly, I want to be a vet. He sucked his teeth for a while and came back with, "had you thought about the shipyard?"

It might have seem absurd but in the late seventies into the eighties, we had virtually full employment. I could have been an engineer, plater or welder, but not it seemed, a vet!

It took me a wee while to accept the situation, but after a few false starts I elected to follow the family route into game and wildlife management which worked for a while, well nearly sixteen years, but somehow it wasn't enough!

A spell at Thurso college had given me an insight to study and research and that eureka moment!

Reading research papers initially of grouse and deer management, the more I read the more I convinced myself that I wanted to be a wildlife biologist and perhaps the next David Attenborough... But I was already committed to roles and responsibilities in my life, I would have to content myself with the wonders of Scotland's wildlife for now.

Personal misfortune and changing circumstance presented me with the opportunity to enter fulltime education, the pursuit of an academic qualification and realising my ambition to graduate as a wildlife biologist. Although by then I had given up on the David Attenborough thing.

At thirty five, university life was tough for me. Once I got a handle on the sex, drugs and rock n roll I seemed to fit in just fine. Well, the rock n roll at least. Like most "mature students" I applied myself and achieved a Churchill Fellowship facilitating study in Africa and America. I met many likeminded inspiring people, land owners/managers, guides, students and enthusiasts so may in fact that it confirmed to me that I wasn't the only one driven by the need to stay close to the natural world.

There have been so many key people instrumental to my journey and personal growth, be they naturalist, conservationist or visionaries.

I could highlight the importance of people like Aldo Leopold, Theodore Roosevelt, George Bird Grinnell and even David Attenborough but I would much rather thank those who were directly responsible.

I have been very fortunate in my career to have had more than one mentor, men and women who guided my career allowing my experience to grow alongside my personal development. Strong characters firmly rooted in the countryside, Len Thain, my first headkeeper, my dear friend, or should that be my "deer" friend Willie Sutherland, my eagle mentor Alison McLennan and, of course, my father.

There are few areas of science more fiercely contested than the issue of what makes us who we are. Are we products of our environments or the embodiment of our genes? Is nature the governing force behind our behaviour or is it nurture? While almost everyone agrees that it's a mixture of both, there has been no end of disagreement about which is the dominant influence.

For me, the nature-nurture debate is redundant! I don't really care why I have a love for the countryside, I just care that it is so. At fifty six, I still don't really know what I want to be (if the BBC are reading this.... replacement for Attenborough could still be an option) I do know that I have thoroughly enjoyed my career and embracement of the countryside. If I could speak with my eight year old self, I would *tell him to follow your dreams.* Your dreams are why you wake up in the morning and try again.

That and spend more time with your father, and accept that he is right. One day you will know why…'

## Simon Whitehead

'Like many others, I look at myself through a completely different set of eyes to those that everybody else does. A product of the industrial North East of England, I am a man that has loved the rabbiting game since I was a boy, and although it has and continues to be hard work, I have managed to turn a hobby into my profession and still keep it my passion.

If I am completely honest, I cannot say why I am so obsessed with ferreting. None of my family hunted, shot, fished or ferreted and I wasn't raised in a rural setting, but the urban sprawl of Teesside. What this did give me was a love of the natural world. As a boy I was fascinated by everything about the great outdoors and I can only imagine that this must have subliminally triggered something.

As a youth, everybody with an inkling of interest in the countryside appeared to have or had a ferret at one time or another. I watched as ferreting became a nursery for country sports. The vast majority of participants left and went onto more glamourous pastimes like shooting or fishing, but I remained loyal to those animals and values that have served me well over the decades and to be fair, I have never seen anything close to enticing me away.

I wonder if it is because I find ferreting holds far more values and principles than just a way of simply catching rabbits. Throughout my half century it has sculptured me as a person, through the experiences that I have endured

84

along my journey, reinforcing that '*dockyard spirit*' that has fuelled my intense drive, that gets me to do what I do, not just for a jolly, but to earn my living. A lot of people want to do what I do, until they have to do what I do.

My world, like my head, is very complex. It is very demanding both physically and mentally, not only to survive but prosper. I have had to become almost chameleon like in many ways, having to learn to think and act differently and to be able to teach myself to do this, I have been forced to delve into differing worlds that nobody would associate me with doing so.

Sporting and industrial professions, pastimes, religions and cultures. Ways of life that have given me the opportunity to cherry pick ideas, mindsets, lifestyle changes, equipment, philosophies and attitudes. If I am convinced that they will help me become better at whatever I have chosen to do, then I will try and if they work, they stay and if not, I put it down to experience and look for other ways.

This allows me to evolve as a rabbiter and as a person, but the one thing that stitches my rabbiting philosophy together is the sobering thought that I am only as good as the animals that I breed and work. I am, at the end of the day, in the result business, and the consequences of being no good and failure are too high to think about.

I am a proud man and my modus operandi is the timeless art of ferreting. Harvesting rabbits using no toxins or poisons.

Managing the land and providing good, clean nutritious food for the table and this marries in with my moral compass perfectly as wherever I find myself, I have the confidence, ability and animals to harvest food for the table. Using good fieldcraft, hard graft, fit, driven animals and a few nets, I can provide a valuable service to those that seek out my expertise, whilst all carried out in an organic and environmentally friendly manner. To the wider world this style may appear primitive, but as I see it, if you cannot better something, then it eventually will age.

If you look back throughout our history, ferreting was the mainstay of those that spent a lot of hours in the factory, mill or mine. That feeling of freedom they must have experienced when they were out with their ferrets is just something, I don't think we can really appreciate enough off today. Over the years that I have spent in the fields of the UK, I have forged many great friendships. Humans, dogs and ferrets have been deeply entwined within the fabric of my life. You can get no better feeling than being in the field with good friends and great animals harvesting rabbits. This could be either ferreting, using lurchers, long nets or indeed bolting rabbits for a uber fast Goshawk or Harris Hawk.

The result is the greatest feeling in the world. That feeling of being able to harvest your own food with your own hands, nets and animals, the provenance of which cannot be bettered. So, you see, to many ferreting may be one thing, but to me it is still everything.

One fear that I do hold is that I feel that within the constraints of the modern world and society, we are losing sight of the humble characters of the land like myself. If we continue to shun and lose characters like me, lose the interaction with the land, if we lose our heritage, what a sad life it would become.

This sobering thought is exactly why we should all believe in environmental responsibility. Not only think very carefully about the origins of our food and the traditional skills required to harvest it, but to educate the world about our world in a way that they would understand. You never know with the way our world is evolving when you may need to call upon those skills and characters like myself once again to provide food for the table once more.'

## Wilma Kass

'I was born at home on a farm near beautiful Loch Tummel, Pitlochry. My parents had five girls and one son all born at home with the local midwife as we were a bit off the beaten track up Glen Fincastle. The midwife used to call my father in and say, 'Bill, I'm sorry but its another girl!' He would have a quick look, say well done to my mother, then go back out to the cattle and sheep!

The winters were harsh but still fun with our wooden sledges and my father pulling us behind the Land Rover. We had so much fun and freedom in my childhood, I never wanted toys as I preferred to be outside where I followed my father everywhere like a puppy dog.

Dad even made me a little stool so I could milk Daisy to get my milk for my breakfast. As I was the youngest I was lucky to be able to do what I wanted unlike my siblings who had to help with all the chores in the house while I played outside wherever Dad was working. He loved stalking the stags as the hills went over to Blair Athol where there were plenty Reds. I was aged five when my mother took me out to stalk a little bit behind my father, just one slow hand down from him meant get down on the ground slowly and quietly. On the way home from school my mother used to take us to the little burn so we could guddle for little fish called tiddlers

The spring and summers were fun as we always had a student nanny come to stay.

My favourite being Hannah from Denmark, so she would look after us allowing my mother to help out on the farm; feeding the shearers who came to help, everyone helped their neighbours in these days. It was fun apart from when my sister fell into the sheep dip at the farm wearing her best camel coat! My mother was furious but at least she was pulled out with a sheep hook and alive! We had a Canadian student who stayed for two years to help my father and he became a family friend and used to send us fur earmuffs for winter from Canada we had never seen them here before. My primary school was on the banks of Loch Tummel with our weekly nature walks through the woods full off wild flowers, frogs, insects it was idyllic really with such happy memories so my schooling was more about the countryside and the wonderful nature and we were taught how to appreciate it and value it at all times.

As I got older, my sisters and brother left home and went onto Uplands College, Bridge of Allan, where all girls learned to cook, clean and Nanny and my brother went to London to make his money and became a very successful businessman. With my siblings leaving home my mother felt rather isolated now there were only two of us at home so we moved to Glenisla and another stunning place to live with my father being farm manager for his good friend John Lascelles senior.

My father's friend had the Glenisla Hotel and we were free to ride his highland ponies whenever we liked while Dad consumed a few drams or more, we fished on the River Isla whenever Dad was free as we were never allowed down to the river on our own.

As I got older the towns or city life never interested me.

Family conversations were always about shooting game and my mother would share recipes for hare, pigeon and venison with my Aunt who's husband was a head keeper at Strathtay. My grandfather was a keeper as were two uncles and cousins .

In my late teens I joined a local rifle club which my father and his good friend were members.  I loved going to the range and trying to beat these two hot shots on a Thursday evening. I realised as I got older I was so fortunate to have lived in such a beautiful place and were taught by my parents to respect all the land, animals, nature around me which myself and my husband have passed onto both our sons.  Its not all wonderful it is very hard work but always worth it in the end.

I went onto meet my husband Lou, a telecoms engineer and great mountaineer and traveller. Lou loved the outdoors and we would camp where he would be climbing with friends and when we had our fist child Ben we would take him in his carrycot camping then came along Niall and they would love to be in our wood with Lou teaching them to cook on slate on a camp fire and talk about all the tales of shooting deer rabbits foxes with my father.

Ben then would go up the hill with his gun as he got older and said he wanted to be a Gamekeeper. Ben went to Strathallan School, we hoped he would become a vet because of his love of animals and understanding of caretaking for the countryside.

Ben shot Clays for his school and was British Independent Schools Champion on many occasions. When watching Ben I used to think there's not many girls shooting Clays. Niall being a keen fisherman when he has free time.

Both our sons loved the outdoors; Niall being very sporty went onto Rannoch school and won many medals for running and rugby. He is also an excellent shot with Clays and game. Niall has his own Landscaping business.

Ben started his shooting business at Errol Park ten years ago, all his family helped out whether beating or picking up and I then went onto cooking the lunches for his clients using the Game from the shoots with my two friends Kim and Fiona helping out. Kim Stewart was brought up in Errol, so she would help beating as she knew the ground and then she got dogs of her own and works them all and beats at other estates now. Her daughter Poppy aged 8 at the time loved going out with Ben on a shoot day listening and learning all the time - it's so important to encourage youngsters.

I prefer game shooting but also enjoy my clay shooting when I have time. I went out on the odd occasion with my husband Lou to local shoots but I had lost my confidence so just used to stay in the background until one day after a family clay shoot I suggested to two of my friends that we try the Clays at Cluny. We got the clay shooting bug, and our husbands had bought us 20 bore Berettas so we didn't have to use club guns. My husband is a member at Gleneagles shooting school and kindly lets me practice there

Cooking the game is so important to us as it is healthy and tasty. I always promote eating game to others that perhaps are a bit wary of the hunting side of it. I always say to try Partridge and Roe as they are not so strong in taste. My favourite recipe is partridge and pheasant marinated in my own Hawthorn jelly overnight, add pan fried red peppers onion and garlic with a little Madeira wine and cornflower to thicken. Light healthy as no fat and delicious. I tend to cook game with a simple home-made jelly in the natural juices roast potatoes and vegetables perfect Sunday lunch

Nothing better than being out on a shoot with family and friends, meeting up with friends from past seasons enjoying the fresh air and exercise no matter the weather and appreciating the hard work all year round that keepers and their families put into the care of the countryside. To the outsider at times it may look like a rich man's playground but that is not true.

The shooting and fishing industry provides homes for families, work for families and most importantly we all take care of our precious countryside.

I now have two little adorable grandchildren so we can teach them the also the love of the countryside that we all share. I am extremely humble having lived my life in the countryside and understanding the hunting of animals and gamebirds and being so resourceful with the meat from everything we shoot as my mother did all her life.'

## Jason Rodd

'It was a fine morning in the summer of 1974, I was 5 years old and I had never been up so early. I happily consumed a bowl of Kellogg's Cornflakes with full cream milk, topped with a tablespoon of sugar. I watched as my father loaded into the car a black leather rod holdall, long keep net and two wicker fishing baskets one much larger than the other.

Alone with my father for what felt like the first time, we travelled down the country lanes headed for Cardington Mill on the Great Ouse just outside of Bedford. The morning air rushed through the open car window and it was fresher and smelt sweeter than I had ever known before. As fields, hedgerows and woodland passed by I noticed that the colours of the countryside are very different at this time of day.

On arrival the car was quickly unpacked and I discovered that the smaller of the two wicker fishing baskets was mine. Despite a considerable amount of struggling on my part I remember feeling very grown up as I reached the carry strap over my head, took on the weight and toddled off behind my father's swaying rod holdall.

It wasn't long before I found myself wriggling around uncomfortably on top of my fishing basket which had been positioned in front of an eddy at the side of the weir. The clean, watery smell that hangs in the air over a weir pool is still one of the most evocative things of my childhood and fishing in general.

I had been away from home almost half an hour and decided it was high time for some sustenance. Opening my creaking wicker contraption, I quickly located a Jam sandwich and a rather exotic, tartan patterned flask inside which I discovered orange squash. The lid of the flask turned into a cup which was something I had never seen before, amazing. I ate and drank as I observed my father assemble two rods, one a fine-looking beast of incredible length and mine, a short stout yellow alternative.

The float my father chose for me was a Perch bob with a dark green stem and crimson red top. I watched as the float with worm dangling someway beneath, was cast a short way out. The rod was handed to me with instruction to strike should the crimson tip disappear. I didn't need telling twice, I was immediately transfixed as the float twitched and dipped on its merry way around the eddy.

As I watched my float complete the circuit for the third time it suddenly jerked downwards then at lightning speed, disappeared beneath the surface. In response to my father's cry of "quick, lift the rod" I hauled with all my might ready for anything that might pull back and attempt to pull me into the depths.

I watched in amazement as my float erupted through the surface like a crimson nosed torpedo rapidly followed by a fat, green fish almost the length of my hand. Both flew well and continued past my head slowly coming to a stop as they wrapped around my father's rod about four feet in front of his reel. Heart thumping, I dropped my rod and ran over to a wonderfully stripped Perch which along with my special float, had spun around my father's line many times ensuring no means of escape would be possible. With a look of triumph beaming from my face I looked up to my father for approval. His brow furrowed and his eyes were closed, he was as happy as me.

My fish was carefully unhooked and rather unceremoniously handed to me. Of course, I didn't notice any lack of congratulatory spirit, I was on top of the world! I had a short time to study the Perch's army like camouflage and very rough skin before it flapped with surprising strength and was airborne once again. This time the fish found a happier landing place back in the river and was gone with a splash.

Despite adrenaline coursing around my body I suddenly felt a prickle in my right hand. Looking down at my palm I saw 4 red spots of blood; Perch have sharp spikes along their dorsal fin. A bit of hardship for sure but how I looked forward to telling my mother about my giant fish and how it had attacked me. I was now a fisherman and will stay that way until I am recycled by earthworms, I hope at least one of which will catch a little boy or girl their very own first fish.

Years have passed since my battle with THE Perch of Cardington Mill as it would jokingly be referred to by family members. Since then I have spent thousands of hours fishing waters as varied as the barren but peaceful Bedfordshire Clay pits to the angry boiling rapids of the

Orinoco river in Colombia. To this day I would just as much enjoy a few hours float watching on a quiet mill pond as I would fighting a mighty Golden Mahseer in one of the raging rivers that cascade the snow melt from the Himalayas into northern India.

It is my 50th birthday this year but as I slip into bed the night before a dawn sortie, I still feel like that little 5-year-old who due to over excitement, woke throughout the night. The fact that I can remember the incident at all but also so vividly, is prima facie evidence something special happens when we go a fishing. I cannot recall anything about the first time I used a computer.

I am usually the driver now, but if it's warm enough I still prefer to drive with the window down and still appreciate that the air has a different quality first thing in the morning. I would rather not reduce this phenomenon to scientific facts. I much prefer the interpretation of that little boy from many years ago; that the sweet smell was the morning magic and it cast an exciting spell.

To the boy this was an adventurous journey along with his father into the unknown. Indeed, to me locations and camaraderie continue to be important aspects of the sport.

I have always loved the excitement of fishing a new water and for the past 20 years "my thing" has been adventure fishing in wild and often hostile locations around the world. In contrast, I have a cousin who has fished exclusively around Bedfordshire and Buckinghamshire for over 60 years. He remains one of the most motivated fishermen I know. Fishing is a very personal thing.

Those first few hours alone with my father was my first experience of the quality time you can enjoy with people whilst fishing together.

The level of camaraderie involved in fishing has changed throughout my life partly dependent on the type of fishing but also as a reflection of what I have needed on a personal level at the time. In my twenties I loved socialising and being into carp fishing provided many opportunities to chat the night away by the lakeside. We fished hard but talked even harder.

When I moved over to Barbel fishing I was at a calmer stage of life and spent many nights alone by the river with only bats, owls and water rats for company.

Perhaps one of the most impressive things about fishing is its inclusiveness. From lofty tarns to inner city canals, no one in the UK is far from a fishing opportunity. Male, female, young or old, weak or strong, there is a venue and style suited to anyone wanting to fish. Almost any level of physical disability can be accommodated, and it can be a very effective therapy for stress and depression. Basic fishing equipment isn't expensive and buying second hand is commonplace for collectors and those on a budget.

Be you Laird or urchin. To stand on some quiet bridge, look down and observe fish glide amongst streamer weed is a wonderful thing. To fish for them might be the most exciting and memorable thing you ever do. If you have never tried, find a friend to take you.

I have never met a man or woman who claimed to regret a single days fishing.'

## Lucy Pitt

'I'm 30 and a forester based in Llandovery. I love being outdoors and found my love of clay shooting whilst at Aberystwyth Uni doing Environmental Science.

However, I shot for the first time with my dad who is a shooting instructor when I was 14 but didn't take it further back then, it wasn't until Uni that I picked up a gun again. When I got to Uni, although I hadn't shot in years, as soon as I saw there was a shooting club I knew it was for me. I joined for the social side and to make new friends. I even roped dad in to coach the Uni team and it went from there. Shooting felt very familiar and I soon wondered why I hadn't kept if going over the years. But at this stage never imagined where it would take me.

Whilst in the Uni Shooting Club I won a gold individual medal at the British Universities and Colleges Sport (BUCS) Sporting Championships in 2009. To be honest that weekend I went along for the social side, just expecting to have a fun weekend and never imagining the result that would follow.

I got an amazing buzz from the win and that is what really sparked my love of competitive clay shooting and I haven't looked back! After the first BUCS in 2009 I competed in two more, gaining two more medals. People call clay shooting is a 'bug' because it catches hold of you and I feel as though my shooting career so far is a true example of that.

Ten years after that random win at BUCS and I am shooting more than ever and totally addicted. I have always been very competitive in any sport I have done, even if it is just a game of crazy golf with friends! Outside the shooting scene I play touch rugby and am in two rounders leagues. I also run and have done two half marathons. I just love sport and being active outdoors.

In 2010 I decided to try and qualify for Wales in the discipline of Sporting. I had friends through dad in the Welsh team who persuaded me to give it a go. I got my first Welsh cap in Sporting in 2010 and later also took up FITASC. On the sporting and FITASC scene I have met some great people. I see the same people year on year in the UK and abroad at shoots. I love being around friends and meeting new people, so clay shooting has been a perfect sport for me. There is a big social side. You also get to shoot in some beautiful countryside around the world with these disciplines. Being a lover of the outdoors this plays a huge part in my enjoyment.

After a couple of years of shooting for Wales I was asked if I would be interested in trying out for the GB FITASC team. The thought of representing GB was so exciting but felt a long way away at the time, but after putting in the work I got my first GB cap in 2014. As you can imagine I was over the moon!

During the shooting season I do as much practice as often as I can and book into as many competitions as I can fit into the diary.

These days there are such a variety of competitive shoots that the diary soon fills up. March to September my life is dominated by shooting but I love every second of it!

Fortunately I have been lucky over the years to get a lot of support and encouragement from family and friends, which has allowed me to pursue my crazy busy shooting career. It is a time consuming sport and that has meant that I have missed things like birthdays and hen dos, but they have always been so supportive and that support means a lot. I have even managed to get a couple of friends into shooting, and as I mentioned before the 'bug' hit them too.

Clay shooting can be such an emotional rollercoaster and have such tight margins, which became very apparent last summer whilst competing at the European Championships in Italy for GB.

We were 21 clays behind the team from France going into the last day of the competition, so realistically thought only silver was going to be possible. I had been struggling and knew I wasn't shooting anywhere near the best of my ability. But after a serious pep talk from my coach and a good chat to my supportive teammates we went back out there on the last day and had a fantastic day and came past France by 1 clay to take the gold! We were stunned. Such a brilliant feeling when digging in pays off like that.

A piece of advice I would give to anyone starting to do competitive shooting is to never give up no matter how big a mountain you feel you need to climb, because perseverance pays off! And it makes those highs feel even better!

I think dad deserves another mention, even now we still set up targets at home that I have struggled with in competitions. I drag him out in all weathers to help me. He is a total rock and has been with me through all of the ups and downs that competing brings. There is a little story I want to share. In 2016 I won the English Open Sporting. I went into the shoot on the back of a few months off from shooting and shot with my dad and a friend just for a bit of practice and some fun. As we were working our way around I knew I was shooting fairly well but had no idea of my score. As soon as I fired my last shot on my last stand dad can bounding over and said 'crikey do you know what you have just shot?!' I hadn't got a clue. I had shot 5 more than the lady who was leading up to that point. He was beaming and he knew I had won it before I did. It was a great day. To do that in a squad with my dad who has supported me so much over the years was a fantastic feeling! I will never forget the look on his face when he told me my score. Moments like that are what drive me on to put the hard work in and help me overcome the lows that are inevitable with any competitive sport.

Since starting competitive shooting in 2009 I have gained 8 caps for Great Britain and 20 caps for Wales.

Along with those caps I have won 6 GB team medals, including a gold in the USA at the World Championships and a Gold in Italy at the European Championships last year. Individually some of my highlights include English Open FITASC Ladies Champion 2015, 2018 and 2019. English Open Sporting Ladies Champion 2016, Perazzi Grand Prix Ladies Champion 2018, UK FITASC Championship Ladies Champion 2019 and I have also been lady runner up at the British FITASC Grand Prix in 2016 and 2018, and UK FITASC Championship back in 2016, and British Open Sporting back in 2017. There is still a lot more I want to achieve, but proud of where I have got so far.

Looking into the future I am hoping to gain further Welsh and GB caps. I absolutely love representing Wales and GB. My dream is to get onto the podium at more of the major competitions for both GB and individually. Also I just want to keep shooting as much as I can and keep enjoying it as much as I do. I have some amazing friends from shooting and just want to keep travelling with them and enjoying my shooting. It is great to share any sport with people that you can have a laugh with. The most important thing about the sport is the enjoyment, so for me being able to share it with friends is a huge part of that. Recently when I won the English Open FITASC I received some lovely messages from shooters who follow me on social media but who I have only met perhaps once out shooting. But it feels like one big family. I have to say I am proud to be a part of the clay shooting family.'

## Kenneth Larsen

'Since an early age I loved the great outdoors. Growing up in Norway with some of the most breath-taking wilderness in the world, it wasn't hard to find places to explore. My first hunting experience was controlling pigeons and crows on farmlands with a powerful air rifle close to where I lived. I was only 14 years old, but this was the beginning of a lifelong interest for hunting.

I was lucky enough to be stationed in the north of Norway during my national service and met up with other guys with a passion for grouse shooting over pointers. Every weekend when off duty, we would pack a rucksack and head for the hills. The interest in shotgun shooting was born.

My early career took me to sea and I joined the merchant navy, travelled the world but had no time for hunting. It wasn't before I married a Scottish lassie and moved to Scotland that I took up hunting again. I got to know a passionate game shooter and we started meeting up for clay shooting and later went out for pigeons and crows.

I was working as a senior executive for a Swedish company and commuted back and forward to Scotland. Sweden has a long and deep hunting tradition and the Swedes are really into their hunting and nature.

With more than 450,000 registered hunters it didn't take me long to find people in my own organisation who shared my passion for hunting. A group of working colleagues decided to enter into a hunting course to obtain our hunting certificates and my interest in deer stalking really took off. I bought my first rife in Sweden and did a lot of wild boar and deer hunting together with a group of dedicated Swedish hunters. To this day, I still hunt in Sweden several times a year and have many good friends whom I met through hunting.

Living in Scotland's newest city Perth, I am spoiled for great places to stalk and hunt. After a career spanning more than 30 years in international business I decided to slow down and spend more time with my family. I started my own hunting business a few years back offering clients fantastic deer stalking opportunities in Perthshire. I have always had an interest in deer management and quickly obtained all the required certifications to manage a well-balanced deer population and the need for crop/woodland protection. Without natural predators recreational and professional stalkers have an important part to play in controlling the deer population. It's estimated that we have as many as 700,000 to 900,000 deer in Scotland. Since the 70's the number of deer in Scotland has doubled.

It gives me great pleasure taking novice and experienced hunters out deer stalking. Today I have returning clients from all over the world who stalk with me. It is a challenging job being a stalking guide.

You need to manage client's expectation and offer a professional service to meet the demand of the clients.

Unfortunately, you meet too many clients totally focused on big trophies and will not take a shot at a nominated cull animal. Every hunter has a dream of shooting a fantastic stag or Roe buck, I get that, but we as deer managers need to get the balance of the deer population right. What a lot of hunters forget is that in 2018 there was 328 trophy Roe bucks shot in Scotland and only 85 made the gold threshold. Out of an estimated 15,000 Roe bucks shot every year that means that you will not find a medal head around every corner.

For me it's all about ethical hunting, fair chase and safety. As a stalking guide, you are responsible for the safety of the guest and the general public. When you meet a client for the first time you don't know what experience and skills the hunter possesses. I will not take a client out stalking if they cannot handle a rifle safely or group 3 shots at a target.

I am particularly interested in introducing new people to deer stalking and getting more women involved. I often find woman more open to guidance and some are excellent shooters. I am also a great advocate for training dogs to find wounded or dead deer. My companion Duke is a Bavarian Mountain Hound and I always bring him when I am out with clients. He gives me a lot of pleasure and is a brilliant blood hound.

A part of hunting deer is handling and inspecting the deer carcass ready for the larder. I love to cook with venison and game. As a trained chef, I decided to launch my own spice range for venison and game under the Venator (hunter in Latin) brand. With the range I wanted to inspire and help people to make tasty home-made sausages, burgers and spice mixes for roasts and stews. We can clearly see that more people are interested in cooking with venison and believe it or not in the UK we have to import venison from New Zealand to meet demand.

Unfortunately, I don't get much time to hunt myself these days but being out in the fantastic landscape here in Perthshire gives me a lot of pleasure. What started as a hobby many years ago has now become my career and I am grateful that I can combine passion with business. My daughter and son-in-law are also engaged in hunting so it has become a small family business.'

## Paul Fenech

'Sea fishing has been my life for the best part of 42 years. When I was nine-years-old, I beached my first ever codling during a winter afternoon session with my dad. That solitary three-pounder had not only filled me with excitement, it had somehow managed to ignite the spark of a lifelong passion.

To be honest, the sea has always been a magnet to me and in those early days, I would spend most of my time on the beach, especially at low tide. I'd find myself scrambling around the rocks hunting hidden peeler crabs, or picking mussels to use as bait. I was in a world of my own.

As a sea angler, it's incredible how regularly and irritatingly, you find yourself constantly checking weather forecasts. Growing up in the North East of England, an onshore gale would suddenly set my pulse racing. This, to a shore angler stepping on to any storm beach meant only one thing...cod!

Little did I know, however, those days (and nights) I spent scraping the mud and sand, turning rocks collecting bait, would in fact turn out to be my first introduction to watercraft.

In my mind, I was imagining fish cruising through the deep gullies I was standing in before the tide flooded them. Cod and bass ambushing sand eels, or snatching a shrimp or a crab that had recently shed its shell. There was certainly more to sea fishing than 'a worm at one end and an idiot at the other!'.

As the fishing bug bore deeper into me, the more determined I was to be a good sea angler. No, hang on…I wanted to be a great sea fisherman!

I read books, bought every fishing magazine on the shelf and learning to tie knots and construct my own rigs. Often, sitting at my desk for hours until I had enough rigs to last me for months. In fact, as many sea anglers will tell you, there's simply no such thing as having 'enough' rigs.

When I reached my teens, my life suddenly found itself being organised around tides. I was actually a decent footballer – an even better cricketer – but I'd regularly find myself on the end of a good telling off for missing practice sessions, or worse, matches. Not to mention the time I failed to turn up on a date with a girl I'd fancied for ages at school. The cod were feeding, I had a fridge full of bait, it was a simple no-brainer…wasn't it?

The fact of the matter is, the only thing that mattered to me was fishing. That feeling I have as I crunch along the shingle to catch an evening tide. Or, huddled under my beach shelter out of the wind and rain, willing my rod tip to pull over as night falls, is simply unexplainable.

This is my world and I love it.

Many of my mates were either sitting at home playing the latest computer game, or watching TV. And there I was, on a deserted beach in the dead of night, doing what I love.

Being the Features Editor of Sea Angler magazine, I've certainly been lucky enough in my job to visit many places around the world, as well as meeting some amazing people.

Whether it's in Norway hunting large cod, coalfish and halibut, or Ireland targeting bass from a surf beach - even in Florida doing battle with a mighty tarpon, I still love fishing and the excitement it brings.

I've caught salmon on the fly in Scotland (double-handed Spey casting can actually become an addiction!), and pike in the Lake District. But, more recently I've found myself falling in love with carp fishing. Some call it 'The Dark Side' but the genuine happiness I have from sleeping in a bivvy, cooking food on the bank or simply chilling with a freshly brewed cup of tea and my feet up, has opened up a whole new world for me.

Finding clear spots, clipping-up to reach the same spot each time, ground baiting at the correct time, it's a totally new ball game to me. It's almost as if I'm learning the technique of fishing all over again.

However, for me, fishing is in my blood and I will never fail to become excited when the bite I'm hoping for comes along. It doesn't matter if it's a drop-back slack-liner from a cod, a subtle rattle from a flattie, a screaming alarm from a carp, or the acrobatics of a jumping tarpon, I still have the exact same feeling of a pounding heart and blood pumping just a little quicker.

I could go on forever, waxing lyrical about how much I love fishing but I've just checked the weather (again) and the tide is perfect for a cod or two, so I'll leave it there.

Oh, just before I go, someone once said to me: "At the end of a tight line, there is always hope!" How right they are.'

## Mark Ancliff

'I was born in a small mining village in Nottinghamshire in 1954, and was brought up on a sporting Estate called Ramsdale. From a very young age, I was interested in the countryside and always had a passion for the outdoors and wildlife. Most of friends pursued a mining career, but I knew this wasn't for me, I used to walk through the woods, about 4 – 5 miles away, to help the local gamekeeper. When I was walking through the woods I came across all sorts of fungus, and different kinds of birds, which inspired me to learn more and find out about each species. I always wanted to be a gamekeeper and I have achieved this goal but I have never looked upon it as a job, more of a hobby. The benefits of being a gamekeeper meant I could study the countryside and all the nature within it.

I left school at 14 years of age on a Friday, and started work at Lincolnshire pheasantries on the Monday. Where I met a man called Ivor Green who was my biggest inspiration, he was a wealth of knowledge and spent a lot of his time with me. He told me stories, of not only, each different type of animal, bird or plant, but also of when he was a prisoner of war, he answered all my questions and as a young lad eager to learn there was a lot.

The woods in Lincolnshire, in springtime, are quite spectacular with the woodland floor carpeted in lily of the valley and bluebells, the buzzing of the bees and the mounds of wood ants which we used to have to dig to get

113

the ant eggs to feed the young grey partridge at the pheasantries.  At this time most of the partridges were hatched under broody hens.  Working at the pheasantries gave me a good stable understanding of country life and work ethic and only encouraged me further to want to become a gamekeeper.

I worked at the pheasantries for five years, and then I was offered a position in Scotland as an Underkeeper at Glen Almond Estate. This was a huge opportunity for a young lad like me, just married, moving away from my friends and family, to start a new life in Scotland.  When I arrived in Perthshire the scenery was breath-taking. The rolling hills, heather and lochs were a vast contrast to the Lincolnshire Fens. When I first a saw red deer and roe deer, eagles, peregrine falcons, salmon and sea trout in the River Almond, I was in awe of all the different species, and I hadn't come across them in Lincoln. I knew I had made the right choice. I lived on the river bank and used to fish the abundant rivers for salmon and sea trout, the rivers use to be full of fish but now I believe the populations have declined.  I learnt  a lot from another mentor, Graeme McNaughton, who taught me how to stalk, to shoot a rifle, and manage and conserve a Grouse Moor.  The first Rifle I shot was a side by side Woodward 303, it was just like firing a shotgun.

I shot my first stag with this gun at very close range, it wasn't very efficient as today's rifles go but we did move on to buy a BSA Stutzen .270 with a scope, which was a big leap forward for controlling the foxes and the culling of the deer. I stayed at Glen Almond for 6 years and enjoyed every minute of it but was presented with another opportunity to further my career which took me to another Perthshire Estate - Dunira, owned By Edward Stanton, who also has a big Farm in Norfolk near Sandringham. My position there was very different to being an Underkeeper at Glen Almond, as I was single handed.

Edward and myself reinstated a pheasant shoot at Dunira, there was also small grouse moor so we had several walked-up days each year. I remember one of my early walked up days, at the grouse, I was out on the hill with 6 Frenchmen, when, all of a sudden, they dropped to the ground, I had no idea what was going on but followed suit, me and my colleague also dropped to the ground, after a moment we realised the cultural difference in that the Frenchmen were going to commando crawl towards the grouse, I quickly told them to stand up and keep walking into them, but each time they saw a covey they were very keen to hit the deck. Finally, we got them to understand the Scottish way and we all had a great day, this is just one of those days that will remain with me. I have very fond memories of Dunira estate as both of my children were born there, but after 5 years I wanted to achieve my goal of becoming a Head Keeper.

In 1985, I was offered a position at the renowned Fasque Estate formerly owned by the Gladstone family, my goal and dreams had been achieved. Fasque is a large estate

115

with tremendous potential for pheasants, red deer and grouse shooting, but also an array of birds, I teamed up with Sam Alexander from the Aberdeen Ornithological group who did an eight year survey of all the breeding birds, we managed to get 95 breeding pairs of resident and migrating breeding birds on Fasque estate: pied flycatcher's, crossbills, corn crake, water rail, quail and many more.

Fasque is where my heart is, the estate offers such beauty, a vast array of wildlife and some of the highest flying birds in Scotland, which have been a joy to wake up to for the last 35 years.

My love of the countryside, its flora and fauna, birds and wildlife, still intrigue and inspire me to this day, and also the joy of telling my grandson all my tales and passing on my knowledge of the countryside to further his passion to follow in my footsteps and also become a Gamekeeper one day.'

## Paul Young

'I think I first became aware of fish, specifically trout, when I was nine years old and playing the part of "Wee Geordie" in the film "Geordie" which was being filmed in the Trossachs. I wasn't needed for a scene being shot so I was standing by the shore of Loch Katrine on a flat calm evening watching ever- expanding circles on the surface. I wondered what was happening, when a chap with a fishing rod hove into view. He cast a concoction of fur and feather onto the surface near one of those circles, gave his line a tweak, and in slow motion the neb, dorsal fin and tail of a fish broke the surface and the concoction disappeared. The angler raised his rod, the fish was hooked and erupted from the water in a shower of spray and was gone. The angler reeled in and as he passed me, he said "That was good fun, eh?" I thought it was brilliant fun and fancied trying it myself…but where to start?

As a family, we went for trips in the car at weekends, usually to the Borders. Living in Edinburgh, Lauder was a favourite spot. My grandfather and his daughter, my mother, were quite keen on 'the fishing' and I was taught how to keep out of sight of the fish and cast carefully. We caught delightful speckled trout, kept a few to be dressed in oatmeal and fried in butter…delicious.

As years passed, my excursions got bolder. I met my lifelong fishing pal, Mike Shepley, and we forayed to the Lyne Water, the Tweed and later to the Tay for salmon.

Our paths diverged often as Mike was a fine sea angler and I stuck to fresh water....and we both were proud to have represented Scotland in our separate disciplines. When Mike was in Norway, he met Ricky Walker, another keen sea angler, and a news cameraman at BBC Scotland. Bemoaning the lack of programmes for anglers, Ricky approached the BBC and we were challenged to make a 'demo'...Ricky filmed it, Mike wrote it and I did the fishing and the chat. It must have been OK, as a series was commissioned. We went on to make four series for BBC, two for Scottish Television and eventually several for the Discovery Channel.

"Hooked on Scotland" was hugely popular, even among the non-fishing community. Ricky, as producer, was always keen for the programmes to reflect fishing in Scotland in a true light. If we had a difficult day, show that - that's what happened. If we had a good day...do the same.  On " Hooked on Scottish" for Scottish Television, we made our first programmes abroad, visiting Iceland and the east coast of Canada, in both places fishing for Atlantic salmon, a fish, after four series for BBC, we knew to be unpredictable. If they were in the mood, we had a chance, if not, we might as well go home...but we didn't, and we caught some fish.

When Ricky negotiated for us to make programmes for the Discovery Channel, well, anywhere there is water, there are fish, and where there are fish, there are people who want to catch them, for food or for sport...or to make

For the love of Country Sports

fishing programmes. We visited the Florida Keys at
Islamorada where we showed bonefish, tarpon and permit
being caught, perhaps for the first time on UK television,
the rocky rivers of the Russian Kola Peninsula, the
Kharlovka and Yokanga where the runs of salmon are
prodigious, to the exotic Seychelles where salt water fly
fishing is a delight, catching blue star trevally. Alaska we
visited several times, on the beautiful Alagnak River, we
caught all five species of Pacific salmon as well as beautiful
wild rainbow trout, on Lake Erie, rainbow trout again and
at the mouth of the Mississippi in Louisiana, we fished
redfish in the fresh water and a variety when tied to the oil
platforms in the Gulf of Mexico.

Central America saw us filming in Costa Rica on a lake in
the shadow of Volcano Arenal…every so often, an eruption
would spout boulders the size of family cars, which rolled
down the mountain into the rain forest, much to the
annoyance of the howler monkeys, who howled!

South America saw us in Chile and Argentina. From
Buenos Aires, a flight took us north to the Esteros wetlands
close to the Paraguayan border where we fly-fished for
Salminus Maxillosus, the golden dorado, a brilliant fish,
and also seen for the first time on British television.

South from B.A. we came to Patagonia and the Rio
Gallegos and a twenty two and a half pound sea-trout and
on the island of Tierra del Fuego, and the Rio Grande, the
best sea trout fishing in the world, one hundred miles from

119

Cape Horn, I caught and retuned my fish of a lifetime – a sea trout over thirty pounds.

Making these programmes has been fascinating for me, different techniques every day, and the most difficult thing? Now, when you are fishing or playing a fish, what is the last thing you ever do? Yes, look behind you…away from the action on the end of your line …but I had to do that all the time, talking to the camera looking over my shoulder. Thankfully, I didn't lose many fish by doing that, and if Ricky was happy, so was I.

I was at a fishing night in Grangemouth a few years ago, when a gent with beer in hand, took the microphone and said, "Paul, a lot of folk here tonight think you are a lucky bu++er, but I know you're not. I know you are a lucky, lucky bu++er"

He's right!'

## Ranald Hutton

'We lived in a country village near a wood and a small river. Having two labradors meant that daily walks in the wood were necessary and enjoyable as there variety in the sounds and sights nature offered.

I always accompanied my Dad in fishing the river, about a mile from the house, was about 10 or 11 and the 'seeds being sown' for my love of the countryside. Dad's love of the country and  fishing in particular it was contagious and each weekend, we piled into the mini and set off for some river in Angus or Perthshire for a day's fishing and picnic.

In those days, you could fish for trout anywhere and they were of a good size. Dad was a good teacher and I learned hoe to fish by watching him. I remember mum cooking trout with mushrooms and tomatoes on the riverbank and it was always a day to remember!

A residential kids angling week opportunity with guest casting instructor Peter Anderson at Rannoch school was an inspiration, not only to be taught to cast and fish by him but to meet other youngsters who were as keen as I was.

Whilst I was attending this, Dad caught his first salmon on the River Ericht and this experience fuelled his angling passion and in turn, mine!

My Dad and I thought we would try fly tying and his encouragement led me to tying flies for the local Dundee fishing tackle shops and also Dicksons of Edinburgh.

Most of the work was for trout flies but Dicksons wanted built wing salmon flies, Jack Scott, Green highlands and Durham Ranger, However, I was often given special orders based on replicating what a customer had brought in – sometimes unusual patterns tied with exotic materials.

At 17 as a professional fly tyer, I won the Fly Dresser's Guild Professional division first place and this success led to many opportunities in the fishing world. These included invitations to fish on prestigious beats of famous rivers which I had only dreamt of previously.

I started tying for myself rather than for shops and demand for the flies escalated. Sometimes it was difficult to keep up with demand and I was tying trout flies at the rate of 2 dozen per hour.

My father also introduced me to Archery and if we weren't fishing, we were shooting arrows at targets in the garden or the woods. I remember, as a rewards for passing my 11+ exam, he bought me a complete archery outfit and this really boosted my interest and progress in archery.

It was target archery which we took part in, attending local tournaments and gradually scores improved.

After I qualified as an Art Teacher a job in Fife necessitate a move there. This was good because we were central to fishing venues and archery clubs.

I worked on my form and mental attitude within the sport and thanks to a great coach in Stuart Henry, was prepared for the toughest competition anywhere in the world.

In 1997, I won the British Target Championships but was keen to try field archery. Progress was rapid and I reached a good standard and inclusion in the Scottish Team, Shooting Home Internationals. Field Archery involves shooting at different sized targets at various distances, set in the woods, over rivers and utilising slopes. A bit like sporting in clay shooting.

I had entered and won most UK competitions within a year and this success coupled with support from family and friends inevitably led to Internals shooting with the Scottish Field Archery Team.

In 1999, my brother also an archer and I, travelled to the European Championships in Germany and over a week of intense shooting at paper targets for 5 days in tricky conditions of dappled light, biting insects and heavy rain emerged as a European champion. This was very satisfying and was the start of my International Career in Field Archery.

The European competition was held annually in various European countries and I always medalled, usually silver and missing gold by a point or two.

I won again in Finland 2003, and the year previously, silver in Switzerland shooting in the Alps. All these experiences were the result of encouragement from my family and friends and also in 2003, I won the World Indoor Field Archery Championships in Zurich!

At the school were I taught, they were so impressed, they put my name on a large wall plaque. Great PR for the public. This in turn was something which promoted me to start a school archery club and in a very short time, led to some promising young archers including area and National Junior Champions!

My life in archery extended over a lengthy period, about 50 years. Latterly, I was lucky enough to be included in the Pro Series, and invitational shoot for the world's best field archers. This was also shot in Europe but the course layouts were very challenging, including such targets as 40 degree or more uphill or downhill shots at distance ranging from 20 – 80 metres, with prize money down to 16th place.

My brother and I had over the years done a little shotgun shooting, mainly pigeon decoying and wildfowling but also shooting clay targets at Game Fairs around the country. He and I shared a love of guns and we enjoyed just looking at the beauty of them as much as anything.

Our occasional game shooting tied in nicely with our love of dogs, having owned labs since a kid. We bought the James Douglas book on Gun dog training and brought our black lab Bess, to a very good standard, she was a very special gun dog! I think we were lucky! A change of direction was needed and interest in competitive archery stopped about 2 years ago, in favour of clay target shooting.

I had some experience of sporting shooting over the years but wanted to try National Skeet, as the targets were reminiscent of pigeon decoying in terms of angles and range.

I had great advice and support from my friends Ian Hutchinson and Robert Purvis, who is now my coach. Others have helped too but I know from my archery experience that one coach is better than twenty! I have in my first year, shot quite well, achieving scores in the mid to high 90s, producing qualifying scores for Scottish Team Selection. It's a new venture and the ongoing experience is generating new friends along the way.'

## Rob Collins

'It all started when I was two years old well almost three, my Father/Grandfather/uncles and Friends were going out traditional ferreting for rabbits, it was near Christmas so must have been December as the decorations were up, I know it was a Wednesday as that was the day the rabbiting club as they called it went ferreting as that was the day they all had off from the docks. My family were all dockers, except my uncle Dave, my Fathers youngest brother, who was a keeper/farmer and had his own land and shoot.

Imagine this, its 5.30am on a cold winters morning, a hard frost outside with a clear sky and a slight wind, now that's proper traditional ferreting weather, purse nets/locators/ferrets and dogs all loaded into Dads old van, this morning I was allowed to go and was my first day in the hunting field, I remember it all so vividly my ears tingling with the bite of jack frost himself, my Mother making sure I was well dressed with my Rupert the bear hat and gloves and some padded suit thing with two pairs of socks on the inside of my Wellington boots. I remember my mother pointing her finger at my Father, saying, I hold you responsible if he gets hurt/lost or covered in mud or anything else.

In latter years, I got the same lecture from my wife about my son, I remember thinking blimey where is the fun in coming back clean, I am sure you folks reading this can relate to what I am saying here.

From that very first morning ferreting with purse net/running dog/terrier and ferrets I was hooked for life, I still say this is my ultimate field sport for I love it with a passion, when I first heard the rumble of the Viking war drums from the Drummers (rabbits) deep under ground doing battle with the Pugs (ferrets) it filled me with such emotions and excitement mere words and pictures do not do it justice, I am still exactly the same now, traditional ferreting laying the nets popping the ferret in and waiting, then those drums start and my heart beats with them.

Moving on later in life, I went to keepering college and passed out a fully qualified game keeper/land and habitat manager and deer manager, I also went on some years later and took a Bachelors degree in coaching specializing fishing and shooting, but my love for traditional ferreting has lasted the test of time 45 years on, I now cover all forms of field sports from ratting with terriers right up to stalking the mighty Stag, it matters not weather on a formal game shoot or stalking the humble rabbit I love all field sports with a passion, my Grandfather a real Countryman of the old school instilled in me from a young age the passion for conservation.

For he always said conservation should be at the core of all field sports, you just cant have one without the other, he also taught me the value of all life, so that he made sure I knew when I took the decision to take a life it has to be for

127

a very good reason, by this he meant for crop/livestock or in many cases wildlife protection, he taught me that every living thing from the crawling insects to the trees flowers fauna and all birds and animals have a right to live under gods canopy, I have tuned this into my cogs in the machine talk when I lecture at college now, I start off with explaining to my students that the Countryside is a well oiled machine and its our job as Countryside Engineers to keep the machine well-greased and serviced but also in good running order, each of those cogs God intended to be a certain size, some big some small, when a wrong cog comes in like say the Grey Squirrel or American Mink its my/your job to take that cog out of the machine, one thing my grandfather taught me was to use the right size hammer (gun) to hit the right size nail (bullet/pellet/cartridge) in the hole, by this I mean don't go using a 308 to shoot a rabbit etc, use an air rifle/22 rimfire/17 hmr or indeed a shotgun, always be as humane and as quick as possible to cull any beast or bird, learn real old world field or water craft too, for the river banks/ponds/lakes and foreshore need our attention and conservation too, I love all fishing disciplines too, long trotting for Roach or Perch, casting a fly rod for Trout/Sea Trout or Salmon on a loch/river or reservoir, or indeed my favourite - fishing for Mackerel with feathers. I love it the most, and fresh Mackerel to eat, ahhhh! food fit for The Gods.

I love just being out there in mother nature, the bag size has never mattered to me it the just being there the rest is all gravy, I also love wildfowling, just imagine there you are out on the marsh the light is just coming up or the sun just setting it matters not as its both magical times, the sound of a distant mallard duck echoing on the wind, the whistle of wings as teal or wigeon zip over head in the almost complete darkness, then the you hear in the distance that ghostly sound of the wild ghost riders the wild Geese, still to this day, it makes my heart pump like a steam train and an icy chill go down my neck making my hairs stand on end, I often just take a brace for the table and just sit and listen and watch the ghostly marsh come alive, or I may join in and practice my game calling.

My Pappy (grandfather) instilled in me a passion for teaching/coaching, I sat and watched him as a small boy to young man, he taught and inspired so many young men and women. He also taught me it had to be done right, he taught me that a love for mother nature and conservation must be the basis of all my field sports, to this day I still pass on my Grandfather's teaching to each and every young sport I coach, I started of Pass It On Young Sports back in 2009 and all these years later this mighty ship made from the finest Somerset English Oak stands tall for all to see, many have rallied to her flag, some have lasted the test of time and are shipmates for life others have jumped ship whilst we have docked at ports around the land.

We wish them well and sailed on, we now have four ships made as strong in our armada, England/Ireland/Scotland

and Wales branches all who sail under our banner with their own flags inspiring their people.

You can see me and indeed my teams representing Pass It On Young Sports at many game fairs and village shows and more around the UK all year round, remember we are all volunteers too so we need you help and support to inspire the Young Sports and their families all about the wonderful world of the Country Sports we all love and cherish, what was passed down from father to son/mother to daughter no longer happens in the right way, kids today are buried with their heads in games consoles whilst parents walk around with their eyes wide shut, so its up to each and every one of us to teach and inspire all about what we love to those Countrymen/women of our future before its too late, as our mantra says at Pass It On Young Sports and I mean all of us for TOGETHER WE CAN INSPIRE.

The true test of a Countryman in my opinion is in your passion for all field sports, your compassion for all living things under god's canopy and to respect mother nature, passing on these teachings from our fore fathers to the next generation, making sure they too have conservation at the very heart of all they do in this wonderful world that we call Field Sports.'

## Rudi Van Kets

'As a little guy, I saw my neighbour at work with his dogs. In itself there is nothing special about it, it wasn't that my neighbour was a hunter with an English setter. Every day I saw him practice with his dogs, at home, in the fields. It could not be left out and when I was 7 years old, the question arose, I would like to go hunting? The beginning of what is still my greatest passion today, dogs and hunting.

As time went by, the hunting bug gripped me more and more. I regularly went as a beater. A few years later I had my first dog, a cross between an English setter and Cocker Spaniel. I tried to copy my neighbour, which sometimes succeeded and then failed, but persevering was the message that I have been trying to give to the students who do an internship every year.

In the meantime, I was already a familiar face among the local hunters. That way I came in contact with a person who did tests with his dogs in Germany. This man would later become my 'hunting godfather'. The fundamentals were laid and I ended up in the world of working dogs.

The first tests with my German Wirehair, Alk, I did at the age of 15. My dog and I were both a pupil between many men with years of experience.

It was not long before the opportunity offered participation in driven hunts in the Belgian Ardennes. Another part, then something very new to me. But I found it interesting, fascinating to see these dogs at work in a different discipline in hunting.

We are again a few years later and I had my first hunting license. I bought a dachshund, Janusz. I practiced with him with the same people who had been helping me for years. In the meantime, we were a trusted and close team. Janusz was a phenomenal dog. I cannot describe how many hours of training there were in this dog, but what I can proudly tell you is that at the age of 18 months we had already taken the tests in Belgium, the Netherlands and Germany. Janusz was the best working dog in Belgium, won the challenge cup in the Netherlands and was twice best working dog of the border region in Germany. This is thanks to a team that helped me with the training almost daily.

I was very interested in one specific part of the tests. The tracking work. I came in contact with people who already had some experience in this domain, they assisted me with the correct advise. I was invited to a driving hunt and maybe I could do a real search with my dog Janusz. I soon realized that the real work is a very different to working on artificial tracks.

I went looking for specialists who could help me better with this something was mysterious part of the hunt; searching for injured game. After all these years, this topic still fascinates me the most. This is my personal preference for working with dogs. I certainly do not prejudice other disciplines within hunting. I am still active in teaching people who want to work with their dogs in the field. I really enjoy seeing these people start training their young dogs and sometimes it just so happens that I see some of them on a hunt.

In the end I found people with years of experience and expertise in the field of tracking work in Hungary. Over the years you build contacts with many people within the dog world. Eventually a meeting followed with until then unknown man to me, meanwhile he is a good friend. This man made sure that I got hold of my first tracking dog, a Hanoverian tracking dog. A dog that was rare at the time in our hunting environment and had no fame. I have to be honest, this dog has pushed boundaries and opened doors.

Thanks to the support of some friends who had experience and knowledge about these dogs, it was just following the directions.
In the meantime, we have been building our own tracking dog group for several years. This led to some very busy years. The reason for this was simple; tracking work was not yet integrated in our hunting culture. We can say that our association for Flanders was the pioneer in tracking work. After all these years we are still busy with this group.

A close-knit, motivated group in which we all strive for the same value, a group that has managed to place itself in the fact that we have been called upon to track lost game for years.

133

The annual training that I give has made many realize that training a dog for the purpose for which he breeds requires a lot of commitment. It is perhaps that inquisitiveness sometimes has its advantages, craftsmanship, knowledge, and sometimes simple tips are then offered by those who have years of experience. This experience comes from those countries that have been working with these dogs for generations and had the opportunity to use the dogs optimally.

Through pleasant contact, the first Hanoverian tracking dogs went to good friends in the United Kingdom, hunters who use their dogs correctly with full dedication and passion. My hope is that these people can get the same amount of respect and there is a bright future for tracking dogs throughout the United Kingdom.

Waidmansheil.'

## Rory Kennedy

'A poignant memory from a childhood zoo trip was a forlorn polar bear. She just stood in the enclosure, swaying her head back and forth in obvious despair. The bear was captive born, she had never known the Arctic, yet somehow knew her existence was unfulfilled; longing for something she had never actually known.

In many ways, we have never had it so good. Most of us will live long, comfortable lives. We are used to instant gratification of on-demand entertainment, retail and knowledge, while airbrushed social media profiles share every detail of our life with several hundred of our closest friends.

But there is something hollow about the modern urban existence. Like that polar bear, we remain constructs of our evolutional environment; millennia living at-one with nature, enmeshed in the constant struggle between life and death. With our sterile consumer lifestyles, is it so surprising that we face such an existential malaise?

For me, hunting provides a meaningful correction to this and so holds a value more akin to a way of life, or religion, than a sporting activity. And like a religion, there are many sects and many ways of practising the same faith. Within our broad church, traditional driven shooting might be the high church, with its baroque garb and practices. Meanwhile the monastic horsehair shirts would be the preserve of the solitary foreshore wildfowler.

135

Yet all of us live by a natural cycle that is attuned to the seasonal offerings and the unique sporting bounty it brings. I live near the estuary and the turning of the leaves has me casting my ears for the first high pitched squeals of the pinkfoot geese returning from their tundra summering grounds. We equate the first frosts with roaring stags, causing the hair to stand on the back of the neck. Summer; we imagine the gentle supping of trout on balmy evenings. Even the hours of the day hold deep significance for us; the expectation of roe bucks in the dawn mist and the singing of duck wings in the evening gloaming. The field sportsman has never lost the connection with nature's cycles and those bounties that once governed our very existence.

I have enjoyed most forms of field sports, each hold a very special place in my heart, but the spiritual theism that holds them together is the concept of the 'hunt'. In this regard all field sportsmen hunt, whether with rod, rifle or bow. It is the act of becoming the predator, and like natural predators, most have their specialist prey and their specialist techniques. It is in the moment of indulging our natural instincts that we are most alive. Tiptoeing through a wood at dawn all the sights, sounds and smells are there to be examined, every part of our being attuned to the ultimate quest at hand.

In its purest form, hunting is a truly wild experience. While I regularly enjoy fishing for stocked fish or shooting driven pheasant, the spiritual side of the experience will always be limited by the artificial premise of these sports. I found my love of fly fishing on stocked trout waters however, I remained enchanted by a local series of wild lochans on a largely unfished marsh system. The floating weed mats were precarious, and you had to regularly reposition as you would soon disappear knee-deep under sulphurous, black bog water. While I enjoyed catching its plump little perch on fly, there were legends that these lochans once held trout but were now long gone. After many months of exploring I hit the jackpot with my first wild brown trout. I still remember my heart in my mouth as I watched it cartwheeling on the end of my line, as I apprehensively guided it away from the weed-beds. By this stage I was already an accomplished fly fisherman and caught a number of specimen rainbow trout from commercial waters however, this little butter-belly was like the crown jewels in my hand and I was awash with emotion as I released it back into the peaty darkness. Wild has a value all of its own.

Another integral tenant is the challenge. The sportsman will intentionally choose tactics that handicap their endeavours, but it is overcoming these self-imposed rules that provide the greatest fulfilment. I have been lucky enough to hunt red stag however, the traditional Highland model neutralises much of the skill of the shooter, being led to a close shot by a stalking ghillie.

On felling my quarry, I have had a pang of remorse, not feeling worthy of taking such a noble beast. I am a regular

stalker but used no more wit or shooting skill than the be-
tweeded tourist stalkers, who invariably don't own a rifle.
Meanwhile I have had humble cull roe out of thick
woodland that has required every ounce of my guile and
cunning and has left my pulse racing with the elation of the
stalk.

I also believe 'interaction' is a closely related factor. Sight
fishing for individual fish is the pinnacle of sport fishing.
With trout it requires you to observe a specific fish and plot
its downfall by 'thinking like a fish'; not by casting at its
swirl but by pre-empting its next rise. Deer stalking on my
own permissions has seen me stalk into bucks during the
doe season, eagerly glassing their movements, knowing I
can target this specific beast come the buck season. Many a
night I have lain in bed thinking about outwitting a specific
buck in this way. On my maiden solo red stalk, I had tip
toed through thick plantation.  As ridiculous as it sounds, I
came to a jarring halt as I could smell the unmistakable
scent of deer. I slowly cast my eye around before making
out the silhouette of a hind through the trees, which I
subsequently shot. Never was I more aware of my senses
and how quickly attuned these become when we are put
back in our natural context. In such experiences we are no
longer third parties, we interact with nature on a far deeper
level than the casual observer; there is an intimacy with our
quarry.

As a continuation of this, taking the animal from the field,
butchering and preparing a feast gives an amazing feeling

of achievement and reminds us of how entwined we are in the process of life and death; a time to be born, and a time to die; a time to plant, and a time to pluck up that which is planted. In evolutionary terms, what more meaningful purpose can we fulfil than hunting to provide food for our families. If evidence were ever needed, you need only look at the brimming pride of a young child proudly bringing home their first bag of mackerel for the pot.

A fascinating extension is the use of an animal to aid our hunting. In my journey I have kept ferrets, hunted with falcons, and worked dogs. To see man and beast interact, each fulfilling a deep-seated instinct, is an intense experience and no relationship is closer than a gundog and its owner. I am currently training a rehoming dog as a deer dog. This pampered pot-licker can be asleep on the sofa but one turn of the gunroom key and there he is, trembling with expectation, raring to go. Wasted by an existence of easy living, he is suddenly lifted, invigorated, and generations of instinctive predatory purpose comes to bare….and when I look into those intense, keen eyes, I wonder if he is thinking the same about me.'

## Mike Shepley

'Entwistle history can trace its origins back to 1895 when Stephen Troughton opened a gunsmith shop in Alfred Street, Blackpool. The name Entwistle first appears around 1930 when Stephen's nephew, Sam Entwistle, took over the business.

Stephen Troughton was my great grandfather. His nephew Sam Entwistle, after whom the company was subsequently named - and their rather nice guns - is remembered with some affection, if not a little awe and trepidation. Sam's chain smoking didn't sit comfortably with a young lad, nor such activities while simultaneously hand-filling 12 bore cases. Sam had survived well enough, as he gave me a photograph dated around 1890 of him packing cartridges and he was doing the same when I visited their gunsmith's premises about 1950.

My father Clifford had absolutely no interest in hunting, shooting or fishing but was a dab hand at drawing and illustrating surgical procedures. He founded the Department of Medical Illustration at Edinburgh University in 1935. I chummed him to his wonderful office at 12 George Square every Saturday morning as I was growing up and proudly sat at his assistant's drawing board, trying to create my own formative pieces of art.

I followed him to Edinburgh College of Art in the 1960s and graduated in Architecture and a post-grad in Town & Country Planning.

I swopped my 410, old rusty 20 bore and rather nice Finnish Valmet 12 bore over and under skeet gun, for my cameras, mainly because I wasn't particularly good at physically shooting things.

The change over was very much confirmed nearly forty years ago when I made a promotional film for Sutherland and climbed the saddle of Benmore Assynt, with an early cumbersome camera and heavy shouldered U-Matic recorder, while filming both stalker and gun. And simultaneously trying to avoid scaring the stags.

Fishing has been my true passion though, something ingrained with the low-water sands on a spring tide at Joppa, on the Edinburgh shoreline of the Firth of Forth.

I was six years old and thrilled at the discovery of setting lines with an older and wiser pal Murray Greenhill. After the tide had receded and we could check the line, it was already dark and we used torches to see if we had caught anything. I felt I was in an Enid Blyton book. Plump lugworm were the hook baits or an occasional strip of salted mackerel which was tougher. We caught plump flounders, translucent dabs and slippery silver eels. Magic.

I cleiked partans from their rocky lairs in amongst the bladder wrack and even simply walking the shoreline where the lines of their submerged shells gave the game away. I was twelve and sold them to Demarco's Ice Cream Parlour on Portobello Promenade. As well as wonderful Ice Cream Sundaes, Demarco's made the best fresh crab cocktails in the whole of Edinburgh. I got a florin a crab, but always kept some back for my mum Sadie. I used the old wash boiler to pop them into the steaming water. humane and far better than as Ive seen touted by some chefs, to let them "go to sleep" by heating the water slowly. Then came codling and mackerel. And of course I discovered wild brown trout and much later, salmon.

In these young exciting days, I had discovered that Sam Entwistle had a wonderful Edwardian house in Blackpool. It wasn't the house that interested me, but the pond at the foot of the garden - my first taste of coarse fishing - diminutive crimson-finned roach, rudd, striped, spiny-backed perch, golden bellied crucian carp and plump medicinal tench.

Mum was thrilled, not with the fishing, but that Frankie Vaughan was also visiting with his young family and sharing the fun. Many years later I co-authored the Guinness Guide to Coarse Fishing with my life-long pal Mike Prichard.

(*NO "T")

Some people will tell you exactly how many salmon they have killed, or as nowadays, more often than not, those released. Personally, I simply haven't a clue, but possibly remember every one of them. Miss Georgina Ballantyne started all the excitement in 1922 at Glendelvine not so far away. Her 64 lbs autumn cock fish remains the British Record to this day.

I occasionally appeared in front of the camera as one of these amateur blokes who pretends to know a little about the country, but mainly to keep an eye on technicalities of tackle and technique. And some of the evening craik and song. We had wonderful shoots spanning the length and breadth of Scotland from the Scottish Borders to Balfour Castle in the Orkney Islands. From seaweed-fed sheep to the Lairg sheep sales.

I met my wife Cheryl more years ago than I can remember. It turned out she's rather good at fishing too. She added an IGFA (International Game Fish Association) World Record to her international title of New Zealand Ladies Saltfly Champion in 2000. Cheryl had already won the Ladies Scottish Open Boat Championship at Lamlash on Arran, but also did rather well at the salmon fishing. Encouraged by our Borrobol ghillie Johnny Hardy, Cheryl was fishing the head of the Manse Pool on Helmsdale in March. And hooked, played and landed a fresh-run 20 pound cock springer. Our dog Halley provided the white hair for a fly dubbed Halley's Comet. The black green yellow and blue layered bucktail wing completed an excellent alternative spring fly to the prolific Willie Gunn designed by that great Brora exponent Rob Wilson.

Rob also crafted wonderful hand-built cane rods: I've still got two.

Along the way, I've made life-long friends and encourage youngsters to discover the joys of angling for themselves. My two sons Chris and Paul have both caught salmon on the fly, in their early teens. They only occasionally fish and that's fine. They married later in life and I'd given up a little on thinking I might have grandchildren. Six years on and I have a wonderful granddaughter and three grandsons. One of my best mates, a lifelong friend was introduced to angling when we were in our early teens asked me at a Joppa bus stop if I was going fishing... well I did have those pull down waders with the studs, a wicker creel, landing net and a rod. We were only kids. He asked if he could chum me the following week and he did.

I love and cherish my fly fishing but competitively, it was sea angling and from boats that attracted my attention. While my old mate Paul did rather well fishing nationally for Scotland after the broon troot. We still fish together, occasionally, but more often blether about the grandchildren.

Quite some years ago, we were chatting having a beer overlooking the River Kelvin in the heart of Glasgow. "I had dream last night" I said. "There were two salmon lying behind that big rock at the head of the pool." "Not in my lifetime." came the retort.

Aye, right!

No time to really mention the change from architecture and planning to film and photography: I've not made my mind up what I want to do when I grow up. More than 20 years in the Middle East looking for among other things Nimr Arabi the Arabian Leopard. Filming archaeologists uncovering an exquisite plaster frieze at a Nestorian Monastery on His Highness Sheikh Zayed bin Sultan Al Nahyan's island Sir Baniyas. The plaster frieze now resides in The Louvre Abu Dhabi.

There was fishing of course in Arabia too, some of it not too far away from Salmon Fishing in Yemen. I filmed youngsters catching wadi fish there. And filming and hunting for houbara bustard and kirwan in Kazakhstan and Pakistan with HE Sheikh Suroor bin Mohammed Al Nayhan and his prized and beloved falcons ,

Tailpiece:

I was privileged to meet and interview David Attenborough 40 years ago, (I used to present a Saturday morning programme for BBC Scotland, mainly about angling). David Attenborough had been a child-hero of mine with his books and programmes Zoo Quest.

Collins had just published his book Life on Earth (1979), republished earlier this year.

I was flying to Manitoba the following day to make a film which I called "Atikameg" - Cree Indian for 'Clear Water'.

I'd made my first film in Orkney in 1968 and was still shooting on 16mm.

Sir David Attenborough is still my inspiration and why I'll be filming wildlife and Nature as long as I can. I mentioned Demarco's Ice Cream Parlour and partans. Richard

145

Demarco CBE is a Scottish artist and promoter of the visual and performing arts. He was born in Edinburgh in 1930. I knew him in the '50s and '60s as Ricky. Richard wrote a book: The Road to Meikle Seggie. You should read it. We all have our own personal Road to Meikle Seggie. Mine went further than the Ring of the North: Canada, Greenland, New Zealand, Europe, Japan and much more recently through five tunnels from Diftah to Khorfakkan.

I do hope yours and mine won't end any time soon.'

## Stuart Dunn

'Gundogs, there are very few hobbies, pastimes, or even professions that can evoke so many emotions within a person all at the same time, other than gundogs. Whether it be the simple natural instinct of being that close to an animal, who trusts you explicitly, and the huge satisfaction that it brings, or the complete opposite and utter frustration, that training a dog to any standard of ability entails, either way gundogs are a fabulous way of energising your mind, your heart and your soul.

I've always had an interest in dogs generally, whether it was the family pet, or the farmer's sheepdog, I always had the notion to have my own dog, and possibly compete at some level in competitions. As a youngster I remember watching the local farmer using his sheepdog to round-up his sheep, and my mind was blown on how this dog can work hundreds of yards away from him, with the only control being his voice and a whistle.

At 19, I applied for a shotgun licence, and as soon as it was granted, shooting became a real passion of mine, and as time went on you very quickly realised that the shooting field would be a far better place if there was a dog to take as well.

That was it, from the moment I got my first spaniel, a Springer called Candy, which I thought at the time, was the world's best gundog until she found out that running after

147

a rabbit was better fun than walking beside me, I was hooked.

From that day forward my passion for owning, training, and competing with gundogs is as strong today as it was almost 33 years ago. My main loves are Springers and Labradors, although there have also been some Cockers along the way too. But, honestly I don't think there are many sports that you can compete in for your entire lifetime, and still be able to pit your skills against the best in the business, and still be able to beat them!

There is something quite brilliant about getting an 8 week old ball of fur and trouble, and in the next 3 years or so nurture it into a magnificent creature, bursting with drive, desire, intelligence, ability, trust, and willingness to please. It can quickly become an "addiction", something that for large parts of your life at least, can start to take over, just ask the many wives, and partners who suddenly find themselves on their own for a night or two each week, because the other half's "training or competing", the weekend that has to be planned around "training", the car that now has to become a pick-up to accommodate the "dogs", the list goes on and on. But one thing is for sure a dog will give you back much more than you can give it.

How do you measure trust, feel-good factor, and companionship, who do you know that would throw themselves in the river in the middle of February, just because you ask them to, who could put a smile a mile wide on your face, and give you memories that will last the rest of your life, and who do you know that can sense the mood you're in, and with a simple nudge with its nose, make even the gloomiest day look slightly brighter, and all for a pat on the head and a kind word or two.

Dogs are a huge commitment, and with average life spans of around 10/15 years, they will have a massive impact on your life, but training for the shooting field, or the competition stages, offers so much in return, whether it's simply a hobby, a way of getting out into the countryside, or getting fitter, meeting people, or even a new career, your life will be a better place with a dog in it. Money, wealth, privilege, standing, materialisms,  none of this matters to our canine partners, for years to come all they need is some trust, guidance, affection, kindness and some TLC, and before you know it, you have a soul mate for years.

When I first started travelling to competitions, it usually meant jumping in your old ex-royal mail ford escort van, with seven million miles on the clock, a hasp and padlock on the back door, and travelling very slowly over Scotland doing nothing for emission pollution in the process.  Its changed days now though, handlers drive up in endless varieties of 4WD vehicles, with the best canine accessories from air conditioning to canine raincoats, silent whistles, noisy whistles and downright ridiculous whistles.

But as the years roll on and the gadgets and add-ons endlessly evolve, one thing has never really changed in all that time, the bond between human an canine must be built if a lasting relationship is to succeed, and that can't be purchased, only created. There is no magic quick fix for it, only time, effort, patience, and creativity and a little knowhow.

The gundog, and probably the shooting field, has changed enormously over the last 15/20 years or so, at one stage it was a rarity to see female dog handlers competing at the top end of the sport, but now more and more female handlers constantly compete for the top prizes, and if you attend club competitions at the weekend, the vast majority of the entrants will be female, and long may it continue!

Clubs all over Scotland, and the UK, need to work harder at attracting young people into the sport, although it is extremely difficult taking into account the cost of dog ownership, feeding, and caring costs etc for young people to start and stay in the sport, but we do need to up our efforts and offer as much support as we can in order to lay the foundations for a stronger future

Some will have gundogs purely for shooting with, some will shoot, and compete in field trials, or tests, and some will be a mix of them all, and a family pet. But whichever field they fall into, effort and dedication will be required in bucket loads to achieve a good level of competition dog, It's not for the faint hearted though, whether it be competing as an individual, or as a team competitor, it's easy to collapse under the pressure of expectation.

It can be hugely exhilarating especially during team, or international team events, when the pressure is on, your hearts trying to break out your chest, your trying not to blink, or even breathe at times, for fear of missing something, suddenly there's a bang, a dummy flies through the air  200 yards away, and on command your dogs on its way, like Shergar out the stalls, through the cover, over the fence, the sweats flowing off your brow like the Tay in May, your mouths as dry as the Sahara, you can barely speak, and wham the dogs nailed it! Scoring 20 out of 20, shear magic!

Unfortunately it's not always good news, the reverse can also happen just as easily, and you wonder why you even bothered, wishing the ground would swallow you up immediately, and save you from further embarrassment. We've all been there, but that's the fun, it really is quite captivating, even on the bad days.

Scotland has long held a great reputation the world over for producing long lines of fantastic gundogs, and handlers, this heritage has taken generations to establish, and some could argue that in recent times we have slipped a little in our reputation. Our country has a history second to none in field sports, with rising standards, unbeatable scenery, unmatchable history, and a sport following which is consistently growing, hopefully the best days are still to come.

So over the last 30 years or so in my life with gundogs, has it all been worth it? You bet!

Some great personal achievements, some national and international competition, some huge highs, some pretty low lows, but many magical moments all created by the simple bond between human and canine, whether you're 8 or 80, it's hard to find something that beats it!

So why not give it some thought and possibly give it a go, it might just change your life.'

## Stewart Robertson

'I was born and raised on farms, back in a time when kids were allowed to wander all day at weekends and holidays without fear. Climb trees, "guddle" for fish in the burn, and use their imagination. It was a great time to grow up. I helped out on the various farms when I was a kid, helping with the hay, harvest, tattie-howking, and trying to help with livestock. Growing up in the countryside gives a person an appreciation of life cycles, predation, countryside management and an insight into how nature works. My siblings and I were part of the land we lived in, earth under the fingernails, wasp stings on the leg, and rabbit on the plate.

My first holiday job when I turned 13 was working on a local farm, driving tractors, topping and rolling grass, gathering hay bales, sorting sheep etc. Thereafter, I was approached by a local agricultural contractor to work with him on holidays and weekends. I did that for five years, then left school to work with him full time. Gathering sheep, lambing sheep, calving cows, trips to the market with livestock, long days at the silage, hay and harvest, driving tractors every day, working with some of the best machinery available at the time. And the constant aroma of silage, cow dung, and diesel from the pores of my skin.

Then. I was guided into the "system".

Apprenticeship, job, always being encouraged to be "better". Once you are in the non-rural system, it becomes a treadmill, always moving just to stay still. Office life, shirt, ties and suits. Progressing to sales, company cars and commission. Don't get me wrong, it was a nice life, plenty travel, planes, hotels and foreign lands. But there comes a time when you look in the mirror and realise thirty years have passed and nothing has changed. Still having to work to pay bills, and little chance of actually "living". Working for someone else, and never quite feeling content. Mortgage, kids, the whole expected life-cycle. I often remembered the days when it appeared that Summers were always warm and sunny, time didn't matter, there were no deadlines, and on occasion, when passing a farm or field, the smell of dung, hay, or silage, would transport me back to happier times. I suppose, if you have lived a life in the countryside, especially a young life, there is always an invisible thread that keeps pulling at you.

Quite by accident, I found myself in a situation where I could help someone who had a lifelong passion for birds of prey. I was asked to carry out some wiring for a local guy I knew who was building his bird of prey centre. I had seen Brian Haining on a few occasions around the area. No one could have foreseen where that would lead.

Once I had done the work required, I helped out with other little jobs. I became really interested in the birds, and was amazed by Brian's passion.

To fund the building of the centre, he held down two jobs, chef during the day, and doorman at night. Pretty soon I was soon handling the birds and flying hawks, helping out most weekends and holidays. The centre opened in November 2004. At this time, Brian's health was suspect. He was having trouble swallowing, losing weight, and was no longer the 19 stone body-building doorman he once was. Then in March 2005, while in hospital undergoing an endoscopy, the probe ruptured his gullet and exposed a tumour, oesophageal cancer. The next eighteen months were an emotional nightmare. We had become pretty close, families became close, and of the friends he had, he felt I was the only one he could really trust.

During this time, he had me handling the golden eagle, Orla. An intimidating prospect, but, through time, she too built a trust in me. I think Brian knew that once that relationship had formed, it would be difficult for me to let it go. Having a full time job it was difficult to make time to get to the centre during the week, however, during his treatment and off days, I had to find the time, either first thing in the morning, or at night after I had finished. There were very few people around he would trust to look after the birds and the centre. When he was feeling down, I would take Brian with me on my trips around the country. We had some weird conversations, mainly about the centre after he had gone. I was sure he knew he wouldn't have a lot of time, the rest of us hoped the treatment would work.

On the 16th June 2006, Brian was told he would receive palliative care. In denial, he tried to convince everyone he would be back on his feet in a few months. He died on the 26th October 2006, aged 41.

The centre managed to survive, just. Closed during the week, masses of work to be done at weekends, it was a real struggle to bring money in, so the hand was dipped in my own pocket. In August 2007, Brian's widow decided she was selling everything off. I couldn't let that happen. I checked my pensions, cashed them in, and bought her out in December 2007.

Through the first few years things went well. However, after being relocated behind the garden centre to allow them to develop a builders merchants, the location and the attitude of the garden centre management soon started to take it's toll. For two years it was a day-to-day existence, never knowing if I could make it to the end of the week. This all affected me and my health.

In 2012 I was invited to relocate the centre to Loch Lomond Shores. Miracles happened regarding funding, and the centre opened on the new site on the 19th October 2013. Since then, things have improved beyond recognition. The centre has a good reputation for standards, welfare, education, and the condition of the residents. Long gone are the nights with no sleep, and the days of counting out 5p pieces to buy diesel.

The centre goes from strength to strength and my health is as good as it could be.

Sometimes I cursed Brian for getting me involved, then I look at what I have now. Working outside every day, watching nature at it's best. Working with some of the most iconic species, getting earth under my fingernails, stings on the legs, and rabbit on the plate. Back to my roots. No days off, no holidays, no social life. Life couldn't be better.'

## Peter Keyser

'It all started when I was ten, shooting my first grouse and catching my first salmon on the Findhorn, a river, surrounded by woods and moorland, featuring much in my formative years and as it still does today. My grandfather insisted that safety and shooting etiquette were top priority; once considered "trained", an outside butt on a driven day was permitted, supervised of course.

So the dye was cast and the spoiling summer holidays in Scotland with my grandfather became the highlight of the year for us young and were repeated over twenty two years, culminating in the purchase of a derelict farmhouse near the river from where we fished, shot and the rudiments of roe stalking were self taught; trial and error (and there were errors!) as there were no roe instruction manuals in those days.

Heady sporting days indeed from which developed a love of the countryside and the birds and animals that were found there. In the south I kept in tune by flighting pigeons on our Cirencester farm roaming with a trusty 28 bore. Grey squirrels became enemy number one and my parent sent me on a trapping course at Cirencester Agricultural College (I was hardly in my teens!)

A spell in the army after school was followed by sporting/ natural history picture collecting and sporting gallery work, alongside many years on BASC Council and Executive Committee, forming the Deer Committee made up of some great deer experts of the day. I set up a gallery in Cirencester, followed by another in London with Farlows all revolving around country sports.

Before leaving London and while working for the Tryon Gallery in London two people I met became life long friends; Rodger McPhail then an aspiring young artist was to become a great sporting companion and raconteur; Brian Booth who ran the Moorland Gallery further fired up my love of roe stalking and had infinite knowledge of sporting artists and natural history. He was responsible for four glorious years fishing the Hofsa River in North East Iceland and a memorable dog sledding week in Norway before he died.

During this period of "sporting work" while still in the south, pheasant shooting took care of the winter months plus a couple of brilliant weeks in Spain. Besides the roe, red stag and hind stalking expeditions seemed frequent, stalking on many estates throughout the north, perhaps the most memorable were the seventeen years in vertical Glen Etive at Dalness under the expertise of Alastair Hunter who taught us so much – "take your time; if this goes wrong, it is 3000ft down and 3000ft up the next beinne!"

Wildfowling became great adventures on the Medway, Cheshire, Anglesey, and Essex (where I fired the first two shots from a punt gun recently built by an artist friend). So much variation in a sporting life.

The family came up to Scotland in 1989 after the stock market crash of 1987; a job running a sporting agency in Perth was offered and agency work continued for a number of years.

Roe stalking proved busy with clients, particularly the drinks nobility from Spain, having access to some good stalking grounds. Another highlight of the Scottish sporting year was the annual February trip to Shapinsay (Orkney), wildfowling below the high water mark which really tested one's thermals and shooting skills. For a number of years house guests and clients were guided after stags in my role as a professional stalker on Scheilhallion and Ardnamurchan – yes, I have all my certificates!

Dogs, in particular springer spaniels, have played a major part in my sporting life. Shooting days are no longer a full time option or affordable but I derive great pleasure in picking up and seeing my team of dogs, the result of generations of breeding, at work.

One of the dogs is trained to stalk with me despite being black and white (my preferred colour). Shooting sporting days and wildlife with a camera has taken over much of my time which I find rewarding; the dogs all too often feature in the winter!

As my parents died when I was still young, my inheritance was to enjoy my sport when I could afford it. I did make the most of it  and do not regret a single sporting day and have so many happy memories; funny how one remembers clearly the days that don't go so well but that's life.

I now hand the reins over to my son who misguidedly is following in his father's footsteps.

I wish him well as I fear for our country sports, blighted by bigotry, ignorance and emotive pressures. I intend to enjoy my days on the hill for just as long as I can.'

161

## Scott Mackenzie

Growing up on a housing estate may be considered not the most inspiring of surroundings for a career in the Gamekeeping industry to blossom and bloom for a young lad, but it was the place where my fascination for all things country sports flourished.

Running through the alleyways, cutting across industrial sites whilst dodging local mongrels kicked out by there owners to do their business, all to get to a local area we called the moat! This place held a fascination to me and my pals as small children. Its mature trees, a pond with an island and best of all, a stream holding countless amounts of stickleback and bullhead fish. With jam jar and nets in hand we'd spend countless hours figuring new ways to drive these monsters of the deep to our waiting nets and then see who had caught the biggest and ugliest looking bullhead.

The mature trees and bushes gave us cover to build dens and lite fires; it gave us a sense of being wild within this urban jungle. Rambo first blood had not long been aired on TV and this made visits to our wilderness more frequent. Inspired by the movie I begged my parents for a "Rambo knife" and that Christmas and to my amazement they did not disappoint. Unwrapping that survival knife on Christmas day somehow gave me a sense of further freedom to explore. So, with my cheap survival knife and its hilt mounted compass that always pointed east, its waterproof matches that never lit and its blade that was so blunt you could slide down it and use you balls for brakes, I would head to the moat to see what that weekend adventures would bring.

As I got older my parents could see that my longing to be connected to the countryside had not diminished, even into my teenage years, and as with all teenage lads, girls, alcohol, good times and cars were a distraction but only ever a distraction from my real passion. The time came during High school when teachers would discuss careers, they had spent the last three years trying to mould us into model citizens and now wanted to ship us off for careers week with the obligatory work placements at the bank, local supermarket or one of the multitude of office blocks that stood tall within our town. The shear dread of being stuck inside looking at four walls prompted my mother to look at alternative work placements for me, and it's my mother I must thank for where I am today.

At a time with no internet my mother wrote countless letters to estate Gamekeepers asking if they could take me on for a week's work experience. I would watch my mom write these letters thinking, "who is going to take on a lad who has more understanding of Islamic prayer being belted out across the school playground from the local mosque than he does of the Gamekeeping industry?" Well a Gamekeeper on an estate not far out of town responded, his name was Michael Addison, and he agreed to take me on for my weeks work experience. The week came and I awoke to heavy snowfall on my first day. My mother was determined to get me there and she did. Pulling up on Mr Addison's drive we were greeted by a man mountain, all kind of thoughts kicked in about this man, "what will he think of me? Will he like me? Will he leave me in the woods if he doesn't?" To my amazement he gave us a most friendly warm welcome and he was quite taken aback that we had made such an effort to battle through the snow to get there as his YTS at the time had not bothered to turn up.

I spent a wonderful week with Mr Addison, I learnt through the week that he had a feared reputation, even to this day people still mention it, but the warmth and encouragement he showed me set me on the path of my chosen career.

From my short time with Michael Addison I went onto spend nearly ten years on a commercial pheasant and Partridge shoot then moving to work on Various estates in North Yorkshire for a further ten years which set the foundations of my understanding of this craft. Through those earlier years I met many wonderful characters and made some fantastic memories with them. Whether it was torrents of tears in the loaders room at some story of a gun who missed most of a particular drive because he was caught short in a hedgerow or the head keepers descriptive look on the face of a long serving beater who had forgotten his wax leggings and realised we were beating the Kale first, all these memory's I will cherish.

People make a landscape what it is, these characters hold a fascination every bit as intriguing as the royal stag I watch holding his hareem on the hill, the sea trout that teases my fly or the woodcock that bursts from the hazel thicket followed by a two barrel salute and my dogs gaze as it continues to jink and jive through the cover.

Now in my 12th year as a Gamekeeper Stalker in the Hebrides I continue to meet and work with some amazing people, I hope one day I can be one of those characters who is regaled over a dram or who has inspired some youngster to follow a path into country sports, just as I was.

## Renato Brodar

'One of the strongest memories of my childhood goes back to the days when I was a small child and my grandfather showed me his revolver. It was a Smith & Wesson 686-3 with a 4 inch barrel and it was extraordinary big for my small hands. I will never forget the feeling when I hold it in my hands. Large, shiny thing made me feel a little bit of scared, but mostly I felt respect and some sort of responsibility. I liked the feeling, I liked it very much.

My grandfather was a hunter before I was born and later, when I showed up, he was no more a part of Hunting society in Slovenia, he simply quit one day. The revolver was one of the remaining things from the old days, like some whistles or similar stuff he kept as memories. I did not know back then that I would also be a hunter one day. Interests or memories of my grandfather really did not played a major part in my life and I think that I was not influenced by any of the people I knew, I was basically more influenced by the nature itself. I loved being in nature, I loved being in the woods and I felt deep respect for the mighty mountains. These are the things that had major impact on me. Also, I liked firearms ever since I remember.

Maybe the love for firearms was much of a reason why I became curious about hunting and then, when I started taking classes and exams about hunting (for getting a hunting license), everything attracted and addicted me so much. The more that I think about it today, the more I believe that you just have to be born this way and bring some of the human characteristics into this world with you the day you are born. Of course later things start getting a shape and the older you are, the more you know about yourself and what you like and do not like, but let's be fair – either you are born with the passion for hunting and you find joy in it (regardless of society, parents, environment,…) or you are not that type of a man. It's either you love it or not – simple as that.

For me, hunting is not a typical hobby like playing some sports or similar. Sooner or later it becomes a lifestyle because everything becomes connected with it. You can play volleyball with friends two times a week, come home, take a shower and forget about it. But with hunting… Oh no, it doesn't work this way. If you are a hunter, a passionate one, every step in your life is affected by it – which type of car will you drive, where will you go for holidays, what type of clothes will you wear, how are you going to spend your free time,… Hunting just becomes a part of you and it affects your lifestyle. The more you discover, experience and learn about hunting, the closer it gets to you and one day you wake up in the morning and realise – this is who I am.

My favourite type of hunting and my best memories are definitely related to the mountains, hunting Chamois in the last days of the year (preferably December and with a little bit of snow). I still feel respect for the mountains, I love

167

silence, the scents, the feeling of wind touching your skin, echoes, rocks and views. Especially the views. And most importantly: in the mountains, I feel free. Away from the civilisation, noise, traffic, mobile phones etc. Simply feeling free being one with the nature.

In my opinion, feeling free is one of the key features of happiness. Mountains often offer a beauty you cannot find nowhere else. Thinking of it, I probably hunt also because of the places it takes me.

Next nice thing about Chamois hunt is that you can do it all day long. You walk or climb to the hunting cabin before evening and get some rest. It is the best if you have a friend along with you. You chat, eat dinner and go to sleep so you are fresh and prepared in the morning. You have to be prepared, because it is extremely physically demanding hunt and you have to be in a good shape. Walking and climbing the whole day somewhere in the mountains is more of a rule than an exception. You breakfast, drink coffee or tea and get ready. You pack your gear, put on your clothes and shoes and… voila! Adventure begins and hiking all day long can start. You observe and spot different animals, you predict weather changes, you cross rivers, paths, peaks and in the end (if you are lucky enough), you choose the right animal and take a shot. Distances are quite long in the mountains because it is almost impossible to come close to the animals, so you have to be prepared and have all the needed equipment with you (laser rangefinder, spotting scope,…) in your backpack.

If the shot placement is perfect and everything goes according to plan, the new adventure begins the moment after the shot. You have to come closer to the Chamois (which usually means a lot of effort and climbing) and eventually take it on your shoulders back to the valley which normally means hours and hours of walking and carrying your Chamois, backpack, water, additional clothes, binoculars, spotting scope, rifle, riflescope, knife, torch, first aid kit,… When you come back to the valley, you feel like you really deserved the animal and it is a nice feeling taking your shoes off, refreshing your face somewhere in the river and enjoy these type of simple, basic and primitive moments which can bring so much joy in a human's life. This is the proper way of learning to respect – respect the mountains, respect the effort, respect animals, respect nature and eventually respect yourself. The days in the Alps are not always sunny and warm and this is what I especially like. Weather can change in a matter of minutes and your hunting trip is always a test of your will, patience and of course, your body. I believe that this is extremely important for a human being – pushing yourself beyond limits which makes you not only becoming better and developing your personality, but also it is the way of how to feel fulfilled.

169

One of my favourite quotes would definitely be:
"Adversity is a man's best friend. Excessive comfort is the enemy".

I especially remember the day when I was hunting a Chamois with a great friend of mine on a hunting ground where my friend lives. It was a harsh day, full of climbing, wind was blowing from all directions and so on, but it was a magnificent day. We experienced amazing views, there were a lot of animals to see (if you knew where to find them) and we had some opportunities, but always something went wrong – position of an animal wasn't right, there where plants and rocks between my rifle and an animal or similar. Long story short, we just couldn't get a Chamois. But we endured, insisted and showed a lot of patience, which paid off at the end. We spotted a pack of Chamois, but didn't have much time before they would hide in the bushes.

We didn't want to lose another opportunity, so we climbed on some rocks really fast (which was quite risky) to get a better view and to come in a position where we could measure the distance and eventually take a shot. Measured distance was 235 meters and I had to shoot at a very steep angle down if I wanted to get a cub. It was an adrenaline rush after hours and hours of walking and it was also quite a test of remaining calm in the next seconds to take aim. Sweat was falling in drops from my forehead and over my eyes directly in the lens of a riflescope so I had to clean it while aiming. What a pleasure it was when we succeeded at last. Thinking of it now, it is a pleasant memory, full of different and mixed feelings, which still amuses me. I am convinced that I will never forget that day.'

## Stewart Blair

'I cannot ever remember a time that I did not want to shoot or go shooting. My Primary 1 report card, states that I wanted to be a Gamekeeper [despite everyone saying that there was no future in it] and the earliest photographs of me are holding a toy gun and quite a few of them sport a dead fox too.

I grew up amongst shooting and spent as much time as I could, pestering my father to take me to clay pigeon shoots [he didn't shoot clay pigeons]. I distinctly remember the night that a local plumber was in our house and agreed to take me along to clay shoots [I think I was about 10]. Mick McAulay was in his late 60s and although he was never a game shooter, he was a great clay shot and travelled the length and breadth of Scotland to shoots, with me by his side. At the same time, I started going pheasant beating, which helped to fund my clay shooting obsession. When not beating or shooting clay pigeons, I was out catching rabbits with my ferrets and best pal Scott or checking lines of fox snares with my father. Fox skins paid for our summer holidays.

Although I was never in trouble at school, it was not a place I enjoyed, so it was a dream come true when I got word that I had secured a YTS Gamekeeping placement! I headed off, aged 16, to my first job at Kincardine Castle in Perthshire. My training also involved placement weeks at Thurso Technical College … little did I know that 25 years later I would be back to lecture there! I then went to Meoble Estate in West Lochaber, where my love of deer stalking was thoroughly confirmed. Meoble was a very special place and rather remote, with no road access, so the only way in was either by boat or boot. Living in a remote location, seemed to suit me, so my next shift was to Loch Choire in Sutherland [which had one road in, 20 miles long]. After that, I jumped between jobs; the then Red Deer Commission, Forestry Commission, Conservation charities and private Estates, but I always seemed to levitate back to the private sector.

I have always been lucky, working with great folk and many characters, all of whom taught me a great deal. I can only thank every one of them for sharing their knowledge and the huge amount of patience that they needed, working with me! I must admit that earlier on in my career, I focused a lot on numbers! Whether it was a grouse bag, the number of heather fires or numbers of foxes shot. In time however, I realised that there was more to life than "the bag" and I adopted a more holistic approach to management.

Nowadays, it is so much easier for people to access information via the internet about all aspects of shooting and conservation.

Obviously, we are all subjected to a myriad of views, but this is what is required in order to form a well thought-out argument. My advice to anyone is; question everything and

173

ask yourself whether you would be happy to be openly questioned on your actions.

I am now a member of a small local syndicate, where we release a few pheasants and have small walked/mini driven days. We do not shoot more than we can eat and really score the day on "the banter", rather than "the bag". I relish these days, shooting and spending time with my friends and family [& poorly behaved dogs]. Visitors to our shoot, get very excited, when they hear us give our sweep numbers in the morning but then realise it is "Bag x Species" [never has a crow been so highly prized!].Oh, and the highlight of the day, lunch - generally game.

The shooting/land management industry has always been under a lot of pressure but right now, it is firmly in the public eye. When, I started out this wasn't the case, it was anti-blood sports versus shooters. Now the issues seem a lot more complicated; upland management, shoot licensing, antibiotic use, poor prices for shot game, raptor persecution and carnivore re-introduction are just a few of the pressures encountered by shooters, hunters and people in the industry. None of the issues should destroy the shooting community, if it is sensible and approaches them pragmatically, however, social media is a double-edged sword, with potential to be used as a positive and negative platform for individuals in the shooting world.

We need to be more switched on, in regard to the use of social media, the number one rule being – if shooting is something you are passionate about, don't give people ammunition to fire at you!

Thinking of a stand out day, is pretty much impossible for me, I've had too many!!!! Whether experiencing the break of dawn, after having sat out at a fox den all night or stumbling upon a coire full of rutting stags – which day would you choose? Getting people their 1st stag is always great, but so is having a dram in the larder after a good grouse day or even finishing off a new line of grouse butts. Looking back, it has always been the people who made the days special and as I stated already, I count myself very lucky to have spent time with lots of inspiring individuals.

Going forward, education is the key, not just for gamekeepers but for all land managers and shooters. We have a great responsibility, not just for the welfare of the animals we are hunting but also the environments that they, and so many other endangered species, rely on. Game management allows these species to thrive, even if many other organisations would rather contradict this. It saddens me, to see other countries where conservation and hunting sit together and are seen as one. Having spent years trying to break down barriers, I think we are now at an important junction, where the sporting sector needs to go forward and identify the failings of many conservation bodies. Is it now up to them to catch up and work with us?'

## Murray Glass

'I started rifle shooting in my teens, then moved to game shooting in my early 30s. My true passion is for being outdoors, seeing the changing seasons, the day moving from darkness to dawn, the peace and tranquillity, the fresh unpolluted air, and taking in all the sights smells and noises around me.

Last year was very successful here at the John Muir Country Park (Dunbar), but what would this year bring? We had long cold spells and snow that brought in good numbers of geese and widgeon last season. This year started slowly with very few Barnies but plenty of Canadas, and numbers of greylags moved from place to place in big quantities.

This year, I wanted to do something different so I moved from my regular areas, this made my things more challenging, with longer walks and earlier rises. This tactic paid off as I found a new favourite spot in the middle of the saltmarsh next to the dead tree that had been brought in by the spring tides. My shooting buddy, William, had found a good spot as well, he perched himself in deep ditch a good 100 yards away, where he could regularly pop up from cover, like a meerkat, to observe birds leaving the estuary.

Mallard flight early most days, in small numbers, and often in the pitch dark.

I would get myself settled in each day with my two dogs, Rowan and Hawke, in their camo neoprene coats, and a flask full of piping hot coffee. It is a wonderful time of day to sit peacefully and take in the sights and sounds of the birds waking up. One morning, not far from us, a fox made its way over the saltmarsh. It never stopped or showed any interest in us hiding beside the tree stump.

As daylight comes in, the first greylags move off at the river and pass over my old favourite spot, couple of 100 move off high over the trees large numbers of pink foot list of that go in the opposite direction probably 2000 head off to the fields to feed. As you sip your coffee, you listen and watch but you never loose your awareness of the time, as the tide starts to fill up the estuary.

A few greylags started to rise off slowly, and instead of following the river they cut across the saltmarsh heading in my direction. Their speed and height increased, around 30 or so spread out in formation. I took three shots, and landed a nice double and sent the dogs out to retrieve the birds. The dogs raced out to pick up the prize, two easy retrieves. I glanced across in William's direction and saw he had also bagged a bird. I packed up my gun, and walked back to the car with William, and felt happy, what a great start to the day. That evening I ate goose burgers with chorizo for dinner, washed down with a beer.

Saturday morning I tried decoying in the local fields, I get up early to pack my hides and decoys: I have build up

177

quite a collection over the years. Once I reached the field, I carefully placed the decoys in a pattern that I hope will attract the geese passing by. It is not long before you hear the 'wink wink' as the birds move off to feed. The first group land two fields away, a good few hundred or so settle in quickly. Large groups of pinks take off, rise and disappear into the distance. It wasn't my day, as I packed up my decoys, the dogs ran about and chased a few pheasants off the field margins.

I ponder what to do next, perhaps an evening flight further down the coast? Later on, I headed for the River Tweed, a beautiful setting next to the arches of the railway bridge. There were plenty of ducks passing by, I take this as a signal for a good evening flight. I heard greylags coming in so I kept myself out of sight in amongst the long grass but they headed up river and slowly turned, and passed just too far away, then dropped down onto the mudflats and settled for the night. As the darkness crept in, I thought the night was over, but I heard a 'honk honk' of a nice group of Canadas about to drop in the greylags but they rose up again, not wanting to share a night with the greylags. They headed over the bay towards the shingle beach upriver. I crouched down as they approach my grassy hide, I lifted my gun and took a shot and I bagged my first Canada, a huge bird and totally new to me. Hawk raced from the hide and into the river, and retrieved the bird from the middle of the Tweed. I sat for a while and listened to an owl in nearby tree, and felt satisfied with my weekend'.

## Rachel Carrie

'My childhood was anything but normal! in the late 80's my father had become successful enough to buy a premises and that's where we eventually settled in a small rural village, the site was set in down in an old quarry and surrounded by agricultural land, bankings and copses riddled with rabbit warrens. the local game keeper kennelled his dogs on our yard. We lived on the yard, our house a very humble porta cabin where mum brought up three children and helped my father grow the business - looking back, I don't think we really realised as kids just how poor we were, because ultimately, we had a fantastic childhood as we lived on a scrap yard.

Growing up we always had a menagerie of pets and animals around, our cabin was surrounded by chickens - my mum is the most caring, nurturing woman I've ever known, the gamekeeper was always bringing orphaned or wounded wild life to her to nurse back to health, one of those animals the gamekeeper brought was a fox cub, which mum hand reared and we had as a pet for years. For as long as I can remember we always had a few good ratting dogs around, the nature of dad's business and the fact we'd inherited the local brewery hops collections as part of the scrap business, meant there was always a healthy rat population to keep on top of.

Ratting was a favourite childhood activity of mine - it wasn't an uncommon sight to see a fox working alongside

179

the terriers. Everything about our childhood was unorthodox.

I was seven when dad brought home our first ferret, a friend of his had a surplus of good working ferrets and so dad brought home a little albino Jill which he gave to my brother. It soon became apparent why this particular ferret was considered "surplus" I remember the blood curdling scream of my brother as he came running into the house with the ferret firmly clamped on his chin! He was a bit put off after that and so the "problem" ferret faced imminent dispatch. I was distraught, I couldn't let this poor creature be killed! I begged and pleaded with dad to let me have a chance to tame her and with that I became the family ferret handler. That little Jill bit, nipped and scratched the hell out of my little hands but I refused to give in, until eventually she did.

I loved animals and I couldn't bear the thought of them being hurt or suffering - a paradox which to this day people don't understand about me. My persistence and love of that little ferret is what led my father on to eventually letting me have my very own small pack of working ferrets, and what bore the very roots of my love of hunting and working the land. My ferret box was an old post box: the strap was the seat belt of an old scrap car. Dad acquired a Harris hawk and I was an integral part of very special team - the team responsible for filling the game bag with rabbits for mums rabbit stew. Dad had a few permissions, one of them was at a local family ran abattoir - the cattle still farmed on site which you don't see anymore since the commercialization of farming, they were overrun with rabbits and so welcomed the pest control we provided.

Rabbiting with dad are really standout childhood memories, I can't think of anything more exciting and exhilarating than scrambling through brambles, ferrets in tow in pursuit of dinner. Dinner that could elude you - and often did. I recall the delight of watching our Harris hawk swoop down on a rabbit that MY ferrets had flushed from their warren, made me beam with pride. Another important role for me was the quick, humane dispatch of the rabbit once it had been caught. I'd been taught to do this efficiently with my priest, from there all the way to skinning and butchering those rabbits on my little butchers block (a tree stump) it was all just a process to me, a very natural process. There was never a need for my dad to be sensitive or censor any part of it from me, I willingly got stuck in from the start. I suppose I was lucky that my childhood exposed me to hunting in its purest form - living off the land and appreciating the natural resources we have around us, back then although it was an adventure, it was necessity and the cheapest way to acquire meat. Also, a fantastic way to teach me responsibility and resilience, and it instilled in me a deep rooted passion for wildlife.

My childhood definitely fuelled the fire that burns inside me to live that life style even today.

As dads business grew, he had to give up the hawk, he simply didn't have the time anymore, despite me being a tom boy through and through my mum had designs on my sister and i being ballet dancers and had enrolled us into the local dance school - those classes turned into a full 5 day schedule of dance lessons of all genres we danced, Irish, Latin, modern, jazz, classical and  contemporary ballet, at weekends we did shows and theatrical performances - despite going on to winning a scholarship from the Royal ballet i stopped dancing in my late teens i still blame all of this period of my child hood for my flamboyance, girly side, my love of fashion and dressing up! - My mum has always been a very glamorous lady, elegant and always well dressed, she's always joked that with my brother she got a boy, my sister a girly girl and with me she got a bit of both! and I suppose that's quite a good way to describe me.

Breaking the stereotype of what people perceive as being a hunter is what has really helped me to inspire more people to give shooting a go, I've proved that it's not just a man's game, its not a lifestyle reserved only for lords of the manor, or the rosy-cheeked farmers sons and daughters.

You don't have to live in a cave and sacrifice modern luxuries, our inherent connection to the land, our ability to hunt, gather and give our food respect and provenance has a real place in modern society. It has a very real place in my home - a real place in my kitchen.'

*Linda Mellor*

About the Author

Linda Mellor, 54, is a writer, and photographer, specialising in country sports, and regularly writes features and articles, for magazines and websites, and is a columnist for Scottish Gamekeepers Association and Shooting Scotland. She is often found outdoors photographing Roe deer and travelling throughout Scotland and Northern England.

Brought up in Fife, Scotland, with gundogs, horses and shooting, her passion for the outdoors ( and hats!) has never faltered.

**Country sports writer and photographer**

www.lindamellorphotography.co.uk

Linda
Mellor

**Fiction author**

Linda is also the author of three novels.

www.lindamellor.co.uk

Cover image photographed by Linda Mellor, wildfowling with Murray Glass and his two gundogs, Hawke and Rowan, Tyninghame Sands, Scotland, January 2019.

Printed in Poland
by Amazon Fulfillment
Poland Sp. z o.o., Wrocław